ECONOMIC CONSERVATISM

American Political Ideology

JOHN A. ORR

Professor Emeritus of Economics
California State University, Chico

ISBN: 1481995979
ISBN-13: 9781481995979
Library of Congress Control Number: 2013901056
CreateSpace Independent Publishing Platform
North Charleston, South Carolina

PREFACE

CONTENT

This book is about ideology, economics and politics in America. It discusses all four of the ideological-political philosophies in the United States today—populism, libertarianism, liberalism and conservatism. The author is a conservative, but is trying to provide a balanced view of all four schools of thought. Nevertheless, the debate between conservatives and liberals is emphasized throughout the book.

This book discusses a wide range of issues, but in essence it seeks to answer six big questions about political philosophy and ideology. This central theme is woven through the entire presentation.

- Why are the libertarians, who have some popular ideas about freedom and the role of government, so unappreciated by most Americans?
- It dominates American politics, the judiciary, the media and academia, but what is liberalism really all about?
- What is civic virtue, why is it so important, and why is it at the heart of the debate over cultural and morality issues?
- Do conservatives really believe in and support something specific or are they just opposed to anything liberal?
- What are the distinct weaknesses of liberalism and conservatism as political ideologies?
- What is ahead for America and can anything be done to improve its future?

This book seeks to add some economic thinking, in the form of a dozen economic postulates, to the political debate between conservatives and liberals. The ultimate purpose of doing this is to show how economic policy in this country can be improved. And every form of policy needs improvement: monetary, fiscal, tax, regulatory, welfare, etc.

This book ends with a personal summary of what the author thinks is most important and wants the reader to understand and learn. The final paragraph is a simple summary statement trying to bring everything together. Some readers might prefer to read the last couple of pages first to see in advance where the author is going. Others might prefer to see the arguments develop gradually towards a final conclusion. Both approaches to the material should work and your personal preference should govern.

WRITING STYLE

I am using an unusual writing style. I find that long passages of abstract materials on ideology, economics and politics can be boring and difficult to read. So I am breaking the material up and deliberately making it somewhat choppy with three devices:

- lots of emphasizing the crux of the major points using font changes;
- using bullets and numbering to keep the major points separated; and
- personal comments, thought starters, and just plain opinions inserted and enclosed in boxes.

Many writers will spend a couple of pages describing something and telling readers the reasons why in a long, flowing narrative. My approach is different. Over a third of a century of teaching, I found that students understood and learned things better when I helped them keep the major points I was trying to get across separate. So my style is to state my case explicitly and enumerate my reasons, making sure to keep each separate concept or argument clear and distinct. The result is writing that is short, concise, full of content, and to the point. If I have done my job, few readers will have difficulty understanding what I am trying to say. That is the benefit of my personal approach to writing. However, there is also a cost, namely that there is a lot of content on every page.

TABLE OF CONTENTS

1. **Ideology:** Introduction to political ideology and philosophy. Introduction to the four American political ideologies: populism, libertarianism, liberalism and conservatism. 1
2. **Populism:** Brief examination of seven American populist movements and populism in general. 7
3. **Libertarianism:** Detailed examination and evaluation of the two types of libertarianism. 13
4. **Liberalism:** History and postulates of liberalism. Key liberal concepts: freedom, equality, justice, virtue, democracy, dissent. 27
5. **Conservatism:** The founding fathers: Edmund Burke and Russell Kirk. Religion and conservatism. General nature and postulates of conservatism. 51
6. **Foreign Policy:** Modern history of American foreign policy. The conservative and liberal approaches to foreign policy. 69
7. **Big Government:** Size, role, functions and growth of the public sector. Limits to the growth of government. The debates over bureaucracy and the size of government. 91
8. **History, Problems, Objectives:** Modern history of the presidency. Liberal takeover of the USA. Long-run problems. Our economic objectives. 107
9. **Evaluations:** Critique of liberalism. Critique of conservatism. Relevant internet fables. 129
10. **Economic Conservatism:** Twelve economic postulates that enhance the understanding of conservatism. 151
11. **Program for America:** Constitutional amendments. Reform of Social Security, Medicare, Medicaid. Changing priorities. Regulation and stabilization. Additional concerns. What we have learned...... 173

A SHORT READING LIST

What follows is a list of a dozen books that have influenced my thinking on American political philosophy and ideology. They are divided into three categories and listed in alphabetic order within each category. Each is full of content and thus informative to read. I strongly recommend all of them.

LIBERTARIANISM

David Bergland; "Libertarianism in One Lesson"; Seventh Edition; Orpheus Publications; 1997

Milton and Rose Friedman; "Tyranny of the Status Quo"; Harcourt Brace Jovanovich; 1983

LIBERALISM

Peter Berkowitz; "Virtue and the Making of Modern Liberalism"; Princeton University Press; 1999

Michael J. Sandel; "Democracy's Discontent: America in Search Of a Public Philosophy"; The Belknap Press of Harvard University Press; 1996

Michael J. Sandel; "Justice: What's the Right Thing to Do?"; Farrar, Straus and Giroux; 2009

Alan Wolfe; "The Future of Liberalism"; Alfred Knopf; 2009

CONSERVATISM

Robert H. Bork; "Slouching Towards Gomorrah: Modern Liberalism and American Decline"; Regan Books; 1996

Jim DeMint and J. David Woodard; "Why We Whisper: Restoring Our Right to Say It's Wrong"; Rowman and Littlefield; 2008

Charles W. Dunn and J. David Woodard; "The Conservative Tradition in America"; revised; Rowman and Littlefield; 2003

David Frum; "What's Right: The New Conservative Majority and the Remaking of America"; Basic Books; 1996

Russell Kirk; "The Politics of Prudence"; Intercollegiate Studies Institute; 1993

Irving Kristol; "Neoconservatism: Selected Essays 1949-1995"; The Free Press; 1995

1

IDEOLOGY

Four political ideologies currently dominate political thinking in the United States:
- populism,
- libertarianism,
- liberalism, and
- conservatism.

This chapter will define each of the four ideologies and show how they relate to each other within two different frameworks. It looks briefly at the American right and the Republican Party, which are much more ideologically diverse and fragmented than the left and Democrats.

FOUR SCHOOLS OF THOUGHT

Republicans are conservatives. Democrats are liberals. This is the common belief in America. It is the generalization used by the media to describe current political thought in this country. It is an oversimplification because there is a continuum of beliefs within each party. Nevertheless, we can identify any individual's political ideology by looking at his or her simple yes-or-no answers to two questions:
- Do you believe that government should play a major role in the economy?
- Do you believe that there should be strong social limits on individual behavior?

There are four possible answer combinations; we can label each:

LIBERALS. YES-NO. Liberals support significant government participation in and regulation of the economy. They oppose most social limitations on human behavior.

CONSERVATIVES. NO-YES. Conservatives oppose government being a major participant in the economy. They support social restrictions on behavior.

LIBERTARIANS. NO-NO. Libertarians oppose significant government involvement and intervention in the economy and most social limitations on what people do.

POPULISTS. YES-YES. Populists support having government play a large role in the economy and society imposing restrictions on individual behavior.

The four schools of thought are in theory distinct from each other, but in practice the economics question dominates the social question. Hence, libertarians are generally thought to be conservatives because both believe that government should play a relatively minor role in the economy. Populists are usually identified as being liberals since they both believe that the government should play a relatively major role in economic affairs.

BRIEF DESCRIPTIONS

LIBERALS favor a capitalistic free-market economy, but believe that a market economy has major problems, especially instability and inequality, so that government intervention in the economy is essential. Liberalism places the individual ahead of society and its institutions, such as religion and families, and thus opposes restrictions on individual behavior imposed by both those institutions and government, except within very broad social limits.

CONSERVATIVES believe that a capitalistic free-market economy is both effective and efficient, while government intervention creates far more problems than it solves, so that such involvement by the public sector is opposed. Conservatism puts society, its institutions and traditions ahead of the individual, and is thus supportive of limitations on the rights of individuals.

LIBERTARIANS put their emphasis on personal liberty. Libertarianism holds that personal rights, including their supporting property rights, must come ahead of all other political priorities. It argues that government participation in the economy and intervention in both economic and social activities should be kept to a minimum.

POPULISTS emphasize the needs of ordinary people and the common man. Populism supports the idea that America's capitalist economy and political system both favor the wealthy and powerful over the little guy. It sees the duty of government as counteracting abuses in both the economic and social spheres.

GO BACK, GO FAST, GO SLOW

There is an alternative way of thinking about political philosophy. How any individual or group thinks about politics, society, and issues falls into one of three different categories: those who want to go back in time, those who want to go fast with change, and those who want to go slow with change. They are very different from each other. Let's look briefly at each.

GO BACK. If you listened to what the libertarian candidate for the Republican presidential nomination was saying in our most recent election, you realize that he and his followers want to go back to a simpler time for America. They want to reduce America's international obligations and bring almost all the troops home. They want to eliminate the Federal Reserve Board and return to a monetary system based upon the gold standard. They want to eliminate a vast array of government participation in and regulation of both the economy and social relationships. In short, liberty is their primary goal and independence from government is how they define and seek to achieve freedom.

Another group, Occupy Wall Street, also wants to go back in time. Precisely what this populist group seeks is nebulous and not well documented, but it clearly desires a return to the prosperous times that existed before the financial and housing crisis of 2008. Such a time had far better job prospects for young people and a lot less government and private-sector money being siphoned off by highly-paid executives in the financial industries.

What is interesting about these two groups is that libertarians are thought to be on the extreme right and part of the Republican Party, while Occupy Wall Street is believed to be on the extreme left and part of the Democratic Party. Yet both are protest movements. If we could get the leaders of both groups together to discuss issues and objectives, we might be very surprised at how much they agree with each other. This shows that political philosophy is not a straight line from left to right but rather a circle where the left and right often come together at the far side of the circle opposite to where the mainstream exists.

GO FAST. The dominant left wing of the Democratic Party, which plays a major role in the party's Congressional leadership and the administration of Barack Obama, typifies those who seek rapid and fundamental change in public policies, and especially those relating to economic issues. They support the nationalization of the American healthcare system. They support significant government intervention in the private economy in an attempt to reduce global warming and resolve other environmental issues. They support major tax increases on upper income groups in order to finance help for lower income groups so as to reduce economic inequality in our society. They are also in favor of the removal of most limitations on social behavior, taking very liberal positions on such issues as abortion, gay rights, and capital punishment.

GO SLOW. The majority of the Republican Party, excluding the libertarians and some others at the far right, fall into the "go slow" category. They realize that the major socioeconomic programs instituted primarily by the left and Democratic Party—Social Security, Medicare, and Medicaid— are exceedingly popular with most Americans and cannot be significantly reduced in scope. They see such programs, however, as being grossly inefficient, costly and counter-productive with far too many negative side effects as unintended consequences. They think of their own role as being one of making government more efficient and effective, gradually eliminating the adverse aspects of most programs. In short, they favor the evolutionary and conservative improvement of existing government programs, in contrast to their liberal counterparts who tend to favor new and relatively revolutionary programs. What this means in effect, is that the majority of Republicans see their role primarily as cleaning up messes left by Democrats.

We still have one protest group unaccounted for—the Tea Party Movement. In part it wants to go back; in part it wants to go slow; it definitely does not want to go fast. It has elements of a right-wing libertarian movement, but it also has elements of a left-wing populist movement. Its primary objective seems to be opposition to anything supported by Democrats and President Barack Obama.

THE AMERICAN RIGHT

The American Right and the Republican Party are identified with each other. In reality, both have numerous parts that are often in conflict with each other. A listing of subgroups inside the Republican Party demonstrates this very effectively:

SOCIAL (TRADITIONAL) CONSERVATIVES. These are usually people who put social issues ahead of economic issues, but primarily believe in strong social limits on human behavior for efficiency reasons.

THE RELIGIOUS RIGHT. These are usually people who put social issues ahead of economic issues, but primarily believe in strong social limits on human behavior for religious and morality reasons.

ECONOMIC CONSERVATIVES (MANAGERS). These are usually big-business people who put economic issues ahead of social issues, but are willing to live with a large government role in the economy so long as they can control and manipulate the public sector.

ECONOMIC CONSERVATIVES (ENTREPRENEURS). These are usually small-business people who put economic issues ahead of social issues, but are especially opposed to government regulation of the economy because it interferes with their pursuit of innovation and profit.

ECONOMIC CONSERVATIVES (POLICY). These are usually pro-business people who put economic issues ahead of social issues, but primarily believe that public policy can and should be made more rational and effective.

NEOCONSERVATIVES. These are usually people who put international political issues ahead of both economic and social issues, primarily in the belief that America should play a major and leadership role in world affairs, even if it has to use military strength to achieve its objectives.

LIBERTARIANS. These are usually people who put freedom above any other considerations in all economic and social issues.

It seems odd to me that the Republican Party is so uniform in its membership but so diverse in its philosophical beliefs, while the Democratic Party is the opposite—quite diverse in its membership but more uniform in its beliefs.

The problem facing the Republican Party and the American Right is obvious from an enumeration of their sub groupings. In essence, there are three interrelated problems:

1. The various subgroups do not agree with each other on many (perhaps most) major political, social, economic and international issues.
2. The various subgroups feel very strongly about specific issues, often taking extreme views about their particular concerns.
3. The various subgroups are usually unwilling to compromise with each other, often feeling that it is "our way or the highway."

For the Republicans to get back in power, they must find a way to overcome these problems and become unified. That will be difficult.

AMERICAN HISTORY

America started out as a conservative nation. There was little government participation and intervention in the economy, and there were strong social restrictions on individual behavior. America stayed a conservative nation for a very long period of time with small government and strong social controls on behavior.

The Great Depression of the 1930s changed everything. In a single decade, public support for a major expansion of government's role in economic affairs multiplied. Simultaneously, beginning in the 1920s, there was a gradual erosion of social limits on individual behavior which has continued to this day, with the 1960s thought to be the pinnacle of this process. Thus, America became a liberal nation characterized by the public sector playing a growing role in the economy and there being fewer and fewer social or government restrictions on what people do.

So where are we now? After World War II, liberals dominated political thought in this country. Conservatives gradually emerged as a counterculture in the 1960s and 1970s. Since the 1980s, there has been somewhat of a balance. For a while, conservatives hold sway, and then liberals dominate. However, it seems that a vast majority of Americans are moderates, neither primarily liberal nor primarily conservative. My reading, nevertheless, is that the moderate middle leans slightly toward being conservative, a little right of the political center.

2

POPULISM

Populism can be thought of in three different ways:
- It is a political ideology that pits the virtuous common people against a dangerous and controlling elite.
- It is a political movement that opposes professional politicians who typically believe they know what is good for the people better than the people themselves.
- It is a rhetorical style of political speech that seeks to represent the beliefs, needs and wishes of ordinary people.

Populism is a popular belief that those with political and economic power, whether in government or business, obstruct the will of the common people. It is the view that those in authority count more than the rest of us. Populist paranoia seeks out and finds enemies of the people; there are always villains, usually in big business or government. A populist movement usually arises from the ground up rather than from the top down; it starts as a popular sentiment and it is only after a while that a leadership emerges.

In short, populism is almost always anti-establishment and antiintellectual. It is a folksy approach seeking the support of average people. Populists rarely think of themselves as populists, but just normal people. Populist movements can fall anywhere on the political spectrum: liberal left, moderate center or conservative right.

HISTORY

THE PEOPLE'S PARTY. The first significant populist movement in America started in response to farm problems in the depression of the 1870s. Farmers formed rural cooperatives to sell supplies to farmers at lower prices, to offer low-interest-rate loans to farmers, and to store excess crops in silos during times of depressed crop prices. The movement formed the People's Party to run its own candidate for the presidency. It supported major changes in the nation's monetary system and nationalization of the railroads. In 1892, it garnered over a million votes and 22 Electoral College votes. In 1896, it combined with the Democratic Party to support William Jennings Bryan, who won over 6.5 million votes but lost a relatively close election. This was the high point of the movement's influence, after which it gradually died out.

There were four significant American Populist movements from the 1960s to the turn of the century:

THE NEW LEFT. In the 1960s, the anti-war New Left took to the streets against what it called "The Establishment" of military, business, and government elites. It was seeking an end to the "imperialist" war in Vietnam. Its disruption of the Democratic Party's National Convention played a major role in the 1968 election of Republican Richard Nixon. Its slogan was "Power to the People."

GEORGE WALLACE. George Wallace, four-term governor of Alabama, formed his own American Independent Party to run for the Presidency in 1968. While he campaigned against liberal reformers and intellectuals, the crux of his program was resistance to racial integration in the South. He won 13.5% of the popular vote and five southern states. His popularity among whites in the South was a significant contributing factor to Hubert Humphrey's loss to Richard Nixon. He ran again in 1972, but an assassin's bullet left him crippled in a wheelchair for the rest of his life.

THE MORAL MAJORITY. In the 1980s, the Moral Majority emerged as a right-wing movement to oppose the liberal elite dominating government, the media, academia, and world of entertainment. Liberals had supposedly created an immoral and licentious American culture. The Moral Majority was successful in changing the dialogue about social and cultural issues, especially within the Republican Party, but its ability to achieve major changes was severely limited.

ROSS PEROT. Ross Perot ran for President as a centrist populist in 1992. He argued that our representatives had sold out to special interests and no longer worked in the best interest of the common people. His program was quite moderate and middle-of-the-road. He believed that the difficulty in Washington was a lack of democracy. His solution was increased democracy through more direct participation in governmental decision-making.

THE TEA PARTY MOVEMENT

The Tea Party was a grass-roots populist movement within the Republican Party during the run-up to the 2010 midterm elections. It was organized locally with no national leadership. Its most popular figure was Sarah Palin, who had been Governor of Alaska and the Republican nominee for Vice President in 2008. Its origins can be traced to a combination of disaffection with the mainstream leadership of the Republican Party and opposition to President Barack Obama and his liberal agenda. In hindsight, it seemed to stand in opposition to eight things (in rough order of importance):

- big government and high taxes;
- large fiscal deficits and the national debt;
- the costly bailout of big financial institutions and big businesses (with little being done for the common people);
- the huge Obama stimulus package of liberal programs;
- the direction the country was going in (especially with respect to cultural, social and religious issues);
- large-scale immigration from Mexico and Latin America (to the point of support for Arizona's strict anti-immigration policy);
- gay rights (and especially gay marriage); and
- affirmative action programs to help ethnic minorities.

The Tea Party was instrumental in the Republicans winning back the House of Representatives in 2010, but that was perhaps the peak of its national influence as it was not a major player in the race for the Republican Presidential nomination in 2012. However, it seems to be much stronger at the local level than in the national arena, having major impacts on many local races. Thus, it should not be written off.

It is interesting that the Tea Party Movement enrolled so many older Republicans who were so strongly opposed to the spendthrift ways and policies of Barack Obama, but who had stood idly by when George W. Bush was running very large fiscal deficits. I wonder how many of these enraged right-wing voters would be willing to give up any part of their Social Security, Medicare and Veterans benefits to bring public spending down to responsible levels and reduce the fiscal deficit.

OCCUPY WALL STREET

In September of 2011, relatively young protesters peacefully occupied a public park in the financial district of New York City. They called themselves Occupy Wall Street and said that they represented the 99% of common people against the 1% of investment bankers, financial leaders, and big business CEOs who were getting rich with government support while the vast majority of Americans suffered. Fairly rapidly, this populist protest movement grew and took over other locations around the country.

The message of Occupy Wall Street was originally vague and incoherent, but became clearer as a general protest against:

- the lack of any significant legal consequences for those who supposedly caused the global financial crisis of 2008;
- the excessive influence of corporations and especially large financial institutions on government policies and regulation;
- the bailing out of giant financial institutions and the automobile industry (GM and Chrysler);
- the large bonuses, amounting to billions, paid to executives and traders in the financial institutions bailed out by government;
- the resistance of top financial executives, who were deemed to have caused the housing and financial crisis, to any government reform and regulation of the financial sector;
- the increasing inequality in the distribution of income and wealth in America; and
- the lack of job opportunities for young people.

The motto of the movement became "We are the 99%." Its symbol became a dancer on top of Wall Street's Charging Bull statue.

I cannot help but feel that Occupy Wall Street would never have gotten off the ground if it weren't for the fact that going to college was becoming less financially and personally rewarding since the 2008 financial crisis, even in such usually lucrative fields as corporate law and business administration. Students had come to believe that they had a right to good jobs after they graduated, but they were finding instead that they were having trouble finding any jobs, let alone good positions.

POPULIST MOVEMENTS IN GENERAL

It is not that easy to generalize about populism in America. My own thoughts come down to a few key words and concepts:

REAL ISSUES. Populism has not been about the little things, but rather about some of the major issues facing our society. Just look at the central issues of the seven populist uprisings we have discussed: farm and rural poverty, the Vietnam War, racial integration, America's moral decay, the proper role of government in a democracy, our ongoing fiscal crisis, and the control of government by business interests. That's a pretty good list.

RAGE. The populists in each of our examples were just plain angry. Albeit about different things, but truly infuriated. It brings to mind the movie scene where a TV anchor says that he's mad as Hell and just not going to take it anymore!

SCAPEGOATS. It is always a battle between the "haves and have-nots." And a few of the haves—a group or a few key individuals—become scapegoats, the target for all that rage.

SIMPLISTIC AND VAGUE POSITIONS. Each populist movement addresses some major problem or issue. Such is easy to define and describe pretty accurately. The suggested cures, if stated at all, are nebulous, vague and indeterminate.

POLITICAL PURGES. Many of the populist movements seek to "throw the bums out." Some want to purge government or just their particular political party of politicians who are not sensitive enough to the public's problems. Others seek to get rid of the moderates who are just not extreme enough to satisfy populist desires.

HOSTILITY TO BUSINESS. The primary villain for most populists is the business community. They believe that big business effectively manipulates and controls our economic and political systems. They believe that big business has too much power to make major economic decisions that affect the lives of many thousands and even millions of people. They are thus ready to believe almost anything negative said about the business community, no matter how exaggerated, culpable and even absurd the statements may be.

By and large, Americans are incensed by the sheer stupidity and irresponsibility of their elected politicians and appointed officials. They believe that the political system is broken and have grave doubts about the economic system. They don't trust government. They don't trust big business. They don't trust the media. They don't even trust themselves. Given the fact that there is a lot of rage in America at the present time, it is highly unlikely that we have seen the end of populist movements in the near future. Whether the next one comes from the right or the left is just a guess. But fasten your seat belts!

3

LIBERTARIANISM

Libertarians are the modern version of the original classical liberals. Their central belief is that the elites in politics, academia and the media all feel that government can fix any of our problems, but the reality is that government interference in the economy and society is the primary cause of our collective difficulties. The heart of libertarianism is personal liberty or freedom—especially from government.

DEFINITION AND CHARACTERISTICS

For the individual, libertarianism is a personal preference for liberty above all other things and objectives. It is the view that you have the right to live your life in any way you choose if you respect similar rights for others. It holds that you should be free to do as you please with your life, body and property, so long as you do not inflict harm on other people and their property. It is based on the belief that people are the best judges of their own self-interest and make the best decisions when they decide freely for themselves.

For society collectively, libertarianism is a political philosophy that advocates limited, constitutional government. Any just system of law and government will supposedly recognize and accept the sovereignty of each and every member of society. As a result, the optimum social-political-economic system is one of individual liberty and free markets with little interference from government.

We can get a better feel for the nature of a libertarian society by briefly discussing several key words associated with libertarianism:

INDIVIDUALISM: The basic unit of society is the individual because he owns himself and has rights.

SELF-INTEREST: People have the right to act in their own self interest, to keep the fruits of their labor, and to do what they want with their property.

RIGHTS: Every individual has rights to life, liberty and property granted by God or Nature, not by society or government. There are other rights but life, liberty and property are the primary ones.

LAW: Social and economic behavior is governed by the rule of law—legal rules that arise spontaneously and are generally applicable so as to allow all of us freedom to pursue our own happiness without interfering with the similar pursuits of others.

ORDER: Social order develops spontaneously and without central direction as if by an invisible hand out of the free actions of large numbers of people.

GOVERNMENT: Governments are formed by individuals to protect rights and thus are limited to only three functions—national defense, criminal justice and providing the social structure needed for economic activity and the enforcement of contracts.

MARKETS: Economic activity takes place in markets that are efficient because they are free of government interference and excessive economic power.

HARMONY: In a just society there is a natural harmony among people who get along with each other by tending to their own business and not interfering with the interests of others. Such harmony and peace extend to societies and nations that do not interfere with and seek to control each other.

LIBERTARIANISM V. OTHER 'ISMS

Libertarians agree with liberals in two important areas of public policy. First, they both oppose government regulation or private institutional control of social behavior, which both consider private to the individual. Second, they both oppose large defense budgets and military adventures abroad. However, libertarians disagree with liberals in three policy areas:
- Libertarians favor a much smaller public sector than liberals do.
- Libertarians want far less government involvement in and regulation of the economy than liberals do.
- Libertarians want to stay out of most international institutions and away from foreign treaties and agreements favored by most liberals.

Libertarians agree with conservatives in three major policy areas: First, they both oppose a large public sector. Second, they both believe in free markets and limited government involvement in and regulation of the private economy. Third, they both distrust most international institutions, treaties and agreements. However, conservatives and libertarians disagree in two policy areas:

- Conservatives favor a hands-on approach to and social controls over individual behavior, while libertarians oppose virtually any social constraint on what people do.
- Conservatives support a large national defense sector that is heavily involved around the world, bitterly opposed by libertarians.

In essence, libertarians are like liberals when dealing with social issues and like conservatives when dealing with economic issues.

TYPES OF LIBERTARIANISM

There are two versions of libertarianism:

- consequential libertarianism—the more pragmatic or realistic version; and
- philosophical or rights-based libertarianism—the more idealistic, pure and radical version.

I think of them as empirical and theoretical libertarianism respectively. Let's look at the two of them separately in detail.

CONSEQUENTIAL LIBERTARIANISM

Consequential libertarianism is nothing more than libertarians using economic cost-benefit analysis to assess in detail all the benefits and costs of a particular project or policy. They will support a project or policy if the benefits clearly exceed the costs, and if it is the best of the available alternatives.

Cost-benefit analysis is used extensively in the business world to assess the profitability of alternative projects and capital acquisitions. Essentially, something will be profitable if the total benefits exceed the total costs. Businesses use this kind of analysis to compare projects and acquisitions with each other to determine the best alternative for investing their capital.

Consequential libertarians use cost-benefit analysis to assess a wide range of public policies and projects. Let's look briefly at how cost-benefit analysis is used in evaluating a new government policy proposal. There are several steps and pitfalls which we can cover in a series of questions:

- What are ALL the benefits of the new policy, both immediate and in the future? Who benefits from the new policy?
- What are ALL the costs of the new policy, both immediate and in the future? Who is hurt by the new policy?
- Can the benefits and costs be quantified into dollar figures? Some can, some can't. Quantifying may be virtually impossible for many things, which can be nebulous and speculative at best. (For example, what is the dollar value of a life saved or lost?)
- How does the potential new program stack up when compared with alternative new policies? How does it compare with the status quo? (Is it really worthwhile doing or would society be just as well off if government did nothing?)
- What else should be included in the analysis? Here you get into what is often overlooked in political discussion because few politicians really care about making the best possible decisions, preferring the politically expedient way out. Nevertheless, here are a few factors that perhaps should be considered:
  1. Public programs usually start small and grow over time.
  2. Costs are always underestimated and benefits overestimated by those who advocate the program and do the analysis.
  3. There often are unintended consequences—positive or negative—of new policies, usually unforeseen by anyone.

The best historical example of an unintended consequence came from welfare programs that provided income for additional children of single parents, which eventually caused the breakup of large numbers of minority families as fathers lost their traditional role in low-income families.

  4. It is very difficult to deal with certain types of costs—human and environmental costs in particular.

5. Long-term costs and benefits are not only difficult to forecast accurately, but also should be discounted back to a present value, using a discount rate that is realistic and doesn't predetermine the outcome. (High discount rates reduce the present value of future costs and benefits to the point of making them meaningless.)

Consequential libertarians generally believe that most government programs, policies and projects fail the test of rationality and can't meet the criterion of benefits exceeding costs. This belief is based on several simple thoughts:

UTOPIAN OBJECTIVES. Many and perhaps most government activities fail to achieve their stated objectives. Far too often, goals are overstated, utopian and unrealistic.

HIDDEN COSTS. The costs of government activity are always understated. Our politicians and bureaucrats have a vested interest in keeping the true cost of the public sector from the general public.

UNANTICIPATED EFFECTS. Many policies have unintended consequences in the long run. It is often better to deal with existing knowns than to face future unknowns, which usually are quite difficult to handle.

INTANGIBLE EFFECTS. Most government activities have intangible and nonmonetary effects. These are almost invariably on the side of costs rather than benefits. Hence, the case for most public sector activities is overstated and far too many of these ventures get through the legislative process.

FEEL-GOOD BASIS. Far too many public policies are supported more on the basis of preconceived notions about their benefits, how they make us feel, and their political attractiveness than on any rigorous analysis of benefits and costs.

WRONG LEVELS. Many government policies should be undertaken, if used at all, at the state and local levels rather than by the federal government. This allows for adjustment to different conditions and experimentation to find which specific policies work best.

ALIENATION. The overextension of the federal government into far too wide a range of activities has an alienating impact on the citizenry because people are having to pay far higher taxes to support far too many programs they dislike. A lot of people believe that there is far too much waste and inefficiency in government.

PHILOSOPHICAL LIBERTARIANISM

American philosophical libertarianism is founded almost exclusively upon the American Revolution and its three key documents: the Declaration of Independence, the Constitution of the United States, and the Bill of Rights (which is contained within the Constitution). Making use of the original wording of the three documents, let us look at some of the key phrases used by philosophical libertarians to support their points of view. There are ten of them:

1. We hold these truths to be self-evident.
2. All men are created equal.
3. All men are endowed with certain unalienable rights; among these are life, liberty and the pursuit of happiness.
4. To secure these rights, governments are instituted among men, deriving their just powers from the consent of the governed.
5. Whenever any form of government becomes destructive to these ends, it is the right of the people to alter or to abolish it, and to institute new government. It is their right, it is their duty, to throw off such government.
6. Congress shall make no law respecting an establishment of religion, or prohibiting the free exercise thereof; or abridging the freedom of speech, or of the press; or the right of the people peaceably to assemble.
7. The right of the people to keep and bear arms shall not be infringed.
8. The right of the people to be secure in their persons, houses, papers, and effects, shall not be violated.
9. The enumeration in the Constitution, of certain rights, shall not be construed to deny or disparage others retained by the people.
10. The powers not delegated to the United States by the Constitution, nor prohibited by it to the States, are reserved to the States respectively, or to the people.

A few of these need some additional explanation. We will expand on five of them but use the original numbering.

1. These truths are self-evident. Libertarians do not have to explain where their fundamental beliefs come from. They are supposedly obvious to any thinking person.
4. Government comes from the people and the people are thus above the government. The function of government is to protect rights. No more, no less!
5. If government turns bad or fails to perform its functions, the people have the right and obligation to change the government, not just the people running it but also its form.
9. Just because some rights of the people were not enumerated by the Constitution does not mean that they are unprotected by the Constitution.
10. Any powers not specifically delegated to the federal government are reserved to the individual states or to the people. The powers of the federal government are limited.

> We should note here that much of what is being said about philosophical libertarianism applies to conservatism in general. The only difference is that most libertarians take these concepts farther and more literally than most conservatives.

FUNDAMENTAL BELIEFS

The following fundamental beliefs apply fully to philosophical libertarianism and only partially to consequential libertarianism:

PERSONAL ZONE OF PRIVACY. Each individual has freedom of action within his own personal zone of privacy. People should be left to solve their own problems in their own way according to their own priorities and values. Thus, each individual is responsible for his own decisions, no matter what the outcome.

NO USE OF FORCE. Nobody has the right under any circumstance to force another individual to do something that is against his or her own self-interest as he or she sees it. This applies to individual action and collective action, including that of government.

FUNCTIONS OF GOVERNMENT. The public sector has only three legitimate functions:

- National defense--protecting the country against foreign intrusion;
- Defining and enforcing personal property rights; and
- Providing the infrastructure needed for the functioning of society and the economy (a monetary system, a system of weights and measures, a legal system, etc.)

Anything else can be taken care of by private interests more effectively and efficiently than if done by government.

NO CONTROLS ON VOLUNTARY EXCHANGES. There should be no legal restrictions and criminal penalties affecting voluntary exchanges of products between responsible people. So long as buying and selling goods and services are voluntary, society and government should not be involved. Even if a vast majority of society finds a product objectionable, possessing that product should be legally and socially protected. This is why libertarians oppose legal prohibitions against drugs, guns, prostitution, alcohol and cigarettes. Only if innocent third parties would be adversely and seriously affected could there be any justification for society interceding in private activities.

DESIRABILITY OF FREE MARKETS. A free market economy is socially desirable because it produces what people want at low cost. No other type of economy is as productive and consistent with individual rights. Supply is responsive and adjusts to changes in demand. Economic freedom is conducive to political freedom and the overthrow of totalitarian governments. People everywhere want free markets and free elections. When people know that they can retain the fruits of their labor, they work, save, invest and innovate more, making themselves and society as a whole better off.

THE THREE NO-NO POLICIES. Libertarians are especially hostile to three types of policies commonly used by governments everywhere:

- redistribution—those that take income and wealth from people with more to give to people with less;
- paternalism—those that seek to protect people from doing harm to themselves; and
- morality---those that enforce the concept of virtue accepted by the majority of society.

Thus it is that libertarians oppose welfare programs, seat-belt laws and anti-prostitution laws. All are considered far beyond the purview of acceptable public policy.

BOTTOM-UP POLITICS. Socialism, liberalism, and conservatism all have top-down approaches to political philosophy. A certain set of common objectives are sought for everyone. Libertarianism is a bottom-up approach because individuals are free to seek whatever they want from society. It is the individual that matters most in a libertarianism political system.

NEGATIVE V. POSITIVE RIGHTS

All rights imply that others have a duty toward the right holder. That duty can be either a negative or positive duty. Negative rights require others not to do something; positive rights require others to do something. In essence, negative rights are those that prevent others from interfering with what you are doing. Positive rights are those that require others to help you, to facilitate what you are doing.

Negative and positive rights are sometimes explained in terms of negative and positive freedom. The former is "freedom from" and the latter "freedom to". The negative right to do something provides you with freedom from interference by others, individually or collectively. The positive right to do something lets you do it, but may require the help of others to get it done.

Philosophical libertarianism is all about negative rights. As a libertarian sees it, people are to be left alone by others individually and society collectively. There are three implications:

- The individual is free to do anything he wants so long as he doesn't interfere with or harm the rights of others.
- The individual is free to do anything he wants with his own property so long as he doesn't interfere with or harm the personal and property rights of others.

- The individual has no obligations to society as a whole so long as he doesn't interfere with or harm the rights of others and obeys society's laws defining personal and property rights. This means he cannot be forced to pay taxes or join the military or serve on a jury and so forth. He can volunteer to do these things, but he cannot be forced to do them.

The bottom line is simply that each man is an island, property rights are sacrosanct, and society has no control over its members.

Why is all of this important? It comes down to the differences between libertarians and liberals. Both believe in freedom, but libertarians believe in negative freedom, "freedom from", while liberals believe in positive freedom, "freedom to." This means that libertarians believe in negative rights while liberals believe in positive rights. For libertarians, the primary right is to be left alone. For liberals, the primary right is to be able to lead the good life. In order to lead the good life, however, society must be involved with the individual, providing the young with education, the sick with health insurance, the old with pensions, and so on. The bottom line is simply that society and government play much larger roles in a liberal society than in a libertarian society.

Let's look more closely at some additional dimensions and implications of positive rights:

COERCION REQUIRED. Positive rights mandate that some members of society do something for other members. Those that are required to serve other members are no longer free to pursue their own personal goals. Some measure of coercion is involved in these duties and obligations. Hence, positive rights destroy negative rights to life, liberty, property and the pursuit of happiness.

STATE PREFERENCES. Positive rights are what society and government want each member of society to have. The values and preferences of the state take precedence over those of the individual. Negative rights are disregarded in favor of positive rights. Society seems to take the view that negative rights are not needed if people can be made happy through socially-provided positive rights.

MORE GOVERNMENT. When society provides its members with positive rights, there is a major question as to which rights should be provided. Is society to provide people with food stamps, health care, housing, pensions, etc.? Which or all of the above? As we move from negative to positive rights, the expected role of government expands exponentially. It is both the loss of the implied independence of negative rights and the vast expansion of the government's social control that is objectionable to libertarians.

TOO MANY SHOULDS. Positive rights open Pandora's Box to different ways of thinking about the role of society and government. People have minimum needs so let's fill them. Some are incapable so let's train them. People would be happier if they had this or that, so let's give it to them. Something ought to be done about such and such so government should do it. The nebulous word "should" becomes the basis of society. This is why we have big government doing so much for us.

DESTROYING FREEDOM. The obligations and duties of positive rights have many dimensions. One group in society has duties towards another. Past generations had obligations to present generations who in turn have obligations to future generations. Everything gets tied together in one big bundle of duties and obligations. This is what a supposedly free society looks like!

The big difference between the two versions of libertarian thought is that the philosophical version comes across as abstract, absolute and absurd while the consequential version is seen as concrete, practical and realistic. It is the difference between being uncompromising and willing to compromise to get something done. To most of us, taxation is not theft and government is not evil. How can you relate to someone who takes such extreme positions? Taxation is the price we Americans pay for our liberty and government does a lot of good for a lot of people. There is no compromising with someone who takes the extreme position that what you believe in is evil and that you must be either ignorant or evil yourself to support it. Political ideology is not all black and white; it is many shades of grey. There is no absolute truth, just a world of opinions.

CRITICIQUE OF LIBERTARIANISM

Most of what the general public hears about libertarianism relates to the philosophical version more than the consequential version. Similarly, most of the criticisms leveled against libertarianism apply primarily to the philosophical variant.

RIGIDITY. When libertarians state that all government programs not designed to protect individual rights are wrong, evil and unacceptable, even those of us opposed to big government find their arguments to be too confining, inflexible and draconian. They leave no room for compromise on their positions.

FOUNDATIONS. Libertarians base their philosophy on the three key documents of the American Revolution, accepting their political principles as absolute truth. Conservatives revere the Declaration of Independence, Constitution and Bill of Rights but see them only as assertions of principle and good guidelines for political action. But these documents are not perfect and therefore they are not the only possible foundation for political decisions and public policy. Utopia, wisdom and perfection didn't occur in the last quarter of the 18th century.

TAXES AS THEFT. Libertarians believe that people have the right to keep all their income for their own personal use and that having to pay taxes is morally wrong. Taxation is equated to theft. Oh, come on! Our ability to earn income is highly dependent upon what government does for us in terms of protecting us from domestic and international threats, protecting our personal and property rights, providing us with social infrastructure (e.g., a monetary and financial system) and physical infrastructure (e.g., highways and public utilities) as well as social overhead capital (e.g., education and health care). It would be difficult to earn an income without government employees and their services, but most libertarians resent having to pay for such. Living in a society is not free and everyone should expect to pay his fair share of the cost of the public sector.

ORIGINATION. Libertarians value property rights and hold them sacrosanct. They think of them in morally perfect terms. They see themselves as having an inviolable right to whatever they receive through voluntary exchange. But where did the right to any specific property first come from? Some native American? Where did property rights originate and could we think of such acquisition as theft that perhaps is not morally justified?

FINANCING. Libertarians leave a lot of the financing of things (from government to assistance for the poor to education to a very long list of socially necessary activities) to private contributions and charity. The adequacy of such an approach is questionable at best. Just look at historical experience:

- People exploit tax loopholes to avoid paying taxes legally, but they also evade taxes illegally in huge amounts. They will go to extremes to avoid paying what we might think of as their fair share.
- Many rich people, landowners and industrialists alike, have lived their lives in great luxury while being totally dispassionate about the miserable living conditions of the lower income groups. Would you have expected financial support from the robber barons?
- Many public goods (roads, schools, utilities, etc.) benefit virtually every member of society and are very expensive, requiring widespread financial support. Yet they are prone to the free rider problem whereby large numbers of people can benefit without contributing to cover the costs.
- Even if an employer is willing to pay his employees reasonably good wages and benefits, competition in an unregulated free market forces him to cut his employment costs in order to stay profitably in business. Economists know this as the competitive race to the bottom.

For these reasons, and perhaps many more, one must question how a libertarian world could possibly be financed.

CONSENT. A libertarian government exists only with the near unanimous consent of the people. Given wide differences of opinion about the proper role of government, even in a society that believes in a very limited role for the public sector, it would be highly improbable, if not totally impossible, to achieve virtually unanimous consent for government to even exist. To say that an implied social contract would exist between the people and its government is unrealistic. To say that people who don't accept the role played by the public sector can leave the country and go elsewhere is even more fanciful in the face of barriers to immigration. Government exists by majority consent, not unanimous agreement.

THREATS. The libertarian concept of negative rights implies that the key threats to freedom come from public interference, violent threats and fraud. But freedom to do what you want with your life is also impaired by other aspects of individual and social life. The former includes differences in health and marketable talents, the latter differences in economic power, political influence, inheritance, education and economic opportunities broadly conceived. Libertarianism is utopian in ignoring the reality of the kinds of lives most of us live in the real world.

INEQUALITY. A libertarian society will inevitably end up with social, political and economic inequality as a result of the oppression of the majority by the opportunistic few who are smarter, stronger and more ruthless. There are two reasons:

- People are by nature selfish, greedy, lacking in self-control and immoral; and
- A minimalist government will neither prevent nor offset the behavior that leads to inequality. There is a trade-off between liberty and equality that libertarians accept but much of society rejects.

THE BOTTOM LINE

Americans believe in freedom. Americans are by and large relatively conservative and opposed to excessive government involvement in markets and economic matters. So why aren't more Americans libertarians? In my opinion, it's really quite simple. When you listen to a libertarian and especially when you read about libertarianism, what you hear and see is so convoluted, abstract and hostile that you want nothing to do with it. If they would just lighten up, more of us would pay attention. We don't want to hear about negative rights, taxation as theft and the illegitimacy of government. We want someone who opposes the expansion of the public sector and higher taxes. We want someone who fights against too much government regulation of the economy and too many legal restrictions on personal behavior. We want someone who has the right opinions but is relatively moderate. We want someone who thinks and sounds like the rest of us.

4

LIBERALISM

Liberalism changes from time to time and from place to place. Always and everywhere the objective is the same—essentially to free the oppressed lower class from the oppressor upper class in order to improve the lower class's lot in life. In Britain and the United States, the birth of modern liberalism in the 18th century involved the middle classes, particularly the owners of small businesses, seeking freedom from an oppressive combination of the monarchy and the church. In the 19th century and much of the 20th, it was more the oppressed working classes, with the help of government, seeking freedom from the oppressive owners of big business. In the latter part of the 20th century into our 21st century, it was ethnic and sexual minorities, again with the help of liberal government, seeking freedom from oppressive white and heterosexual majorities. So it was that liberals started out wanting to reduce the role and power of the state but ended up wanting the public sector to have a bigger role to counter the economic power of the business sector or social power of the political majority.

Don't be put off by my using the politically sensitive terms of oppressed and oppressor; this is the way the supposedly oppressed think about their situation. You and I might disagree with the way they think, but that doesn't alter the fact of their feeling oppressed.

In modern times we can see major differences in liberal uprisings from country to country. The liberal uprisings against Marxist Communism in Poland and much of Eastern Europe had the church heavily involved in the battle against a secular government. Yet in Afghanistan, it was secular interests rising up against a very doctrinaire Muslim government. The nature of liberalism varies from country to country and from generation to generation. What remains the same is the quest for freedom.

The Golden Age of American Liberalism started in 1933 with the Democratic administration of President Franklin D. Roosevelt. It lasted approximately four decades into the 1970s. It featured Roosevelt's New Deal at the beginning and President Lyndon Johnson's Great Society at the end. It spawned the movement era. Such started with the civil rights movement and Martin Luther King. It continued with the antiwar crusade against the Viet Nam War. Then we saw the beginnings of three other movements that have continued to this day: environmentalism, women's liberation and gay liberation. Liberals and the Democratic Party dominated our politics, controlling the Presidency, Senate and House of Representatives most of the time. Liberals also dominated the intellectual climate— the universities, the media, and the movie industry—with conservatives few and far between.

In many senses of the word, we are all liberals now. Liberal programs and policies have been accepted by almost everyone. Social Security and Medicare—programs for the old—are so sacrosanct that they have been called the third rail of American politics, untouchable by either political party in spite of the fact that both need change before they become too fragile financially. Much the same could be said about Medicaid and welfare—our programs for the poor. We all accept the need for environmental restraint. The rights of ethnic minorities, women and gays are well recognized not just in law but also in practice. The attitudes of most Americans are more liberal now than they were in past generations. In short, liberalism has succeeded and dominates the American way of life. Sure, conservatives rant about what they see as the excesses of liberalism. The truth is, however, that they accept the vast majority of what liberalism has wrought. They don't want to change the fundamental nature of American society, fully aware that voters would not allow them to do so anyway. They rather hope to fine tune things and make the American good life even better.

GENERAL NATURE AND DEFINITION

There is no single accepted definition of liberalism. So let us look at what liberalism entails before turning to the best available definition. With some elaboration added, liberalism is:

- a political theory based on the beliefs that people are by nature good, and that they learn and thus improve over time;
- a political philosophy the puts the individual before the family, community, society, state or government;
- a social philosophy that has the equality of all mankind as its primary and ultimate objective, and seeks to achieve such equality through the freedom of and justice for all;

> This explains why the three concepts of equality, freedom and justice are used almost interchangeably in liberal thought.

- a doctrine of rights, one that states that people have inalienable rights including but not limited to freedom of thought and speech, freedom of religion, freedom of association, freedom from want, the right to due process, the right to vote, and the right to own property;
- an economic philosophy that favors capitalism, free markets, competition, and minimal government involvement in and regulation of the economy;
- a belief in evolutionary reform in moral, religious, social, economic and political concerns;
- an approach to social and political revolution against all forms of oppressive and totalitarian governments; and
- a theory of government stressing constitutional limits to government action, separation of powers, and representation.

Perhaps the best discussion of how to define liberalism was that of Alan Wolfe.[1] His definition had three distinct parts:

- the substance of liberalism;
- the procedures of liberalism; and
- the temperament of liberalism.

Following Wolfe's reasoning, let's briefly examine each in turn.

SUBSTANCE: The fundamental substantive principle of liberalism is that people should be enabled and allowed to control the directions their lives take. This requires freedom to make their own choices—both negative freedom from external restraints and positive freedom to be able to do what they want to do. But freedom implies that there must be some minimal degree of equality to allow people to have a reasonable range of alternative opportunities from which to choose. Hence, the substantive aspect of liberalism puts emphasis on both freedom and equality.

PROCEDURE: The paramount procedural principle of liberalism is to use fair and impartial rules to settle disagreements among competing interest groups. The approach used in most democracies is constitutional government that tries to treat everyone the same without exception. For procedural justice to prevail, it is especially important that the rules apply not only to the people but also to the government and its leaders.

TEMPERAMENT: The liberal temperament has more to do with how ideas are approached then with the ideas themselves. It relates to one's disposition, spirit and psyche. To be liberal, you should be tolerant to those who oppose you, moderate and hostile to extreme views, open-minded and receptive to new ideas, caring and humane for those worse off than you are, and willing to work for what you believe in.

THE POSTULATES OF LIBERALISM

Liberalism can be described in terms of a series of postulates, essentially fundamental statements about what liberalism is and what liberals believe. We call these statements postulates because they are accepted by liberals as the truth without proof. What follows is my personal attempt to describe the essence of liberalism—what liberalism is and what liberals believe. There are an even dozen postulates, each given a descriptive title. There are also twelve very different postulates of conservatism to be discussed in the next chapter.

HUMAN NATURE. People are inherently good, kind, decent and personable. With proper education and social involvement, over time mankind naturally improves, both individually and collectively. There is thus an inherent tendency toward progress in society.

THE INDIVIDUAL'S RATIONALITY. People are intelligent and logical. Thus, human reason and rational science can not only understand the world but also solve its problems. Since solutions to society's difficulties exist, progress and reform are possible.

MORALITY. Moral standards are relative to the nature of society, localized to each community, and subjective to the individual. They are modifiable to fit different situations. They are not absolutes provided to mankind by divine revelation or natural history, but are a product of human reason.

CHANGE. Social change should not be so rapid and revolutionary as to be disruptive, but society must steadily change and evolve to avoid becoming stagnant and restraining.

CAPITALISM. Capitalism is a good and viable economic system, but it is prone to inequality, instability, insecurity, and the inefficiency created by monopoly power and the disregard of social costs. Thus, extensive government involvement in and regulation of the private sector of the economy is required.

EQUALITY. Complete equality in economic, social and political outcomes is impossible to achieve, but society should strive toward greater equality because it not only reduces hostility between and separation of the classes, but also enhances personal freedom and promotes self development.

DEMOCRACY. The will of the majority of society should prevail in a democracy that is responsive to changing social needs and attitudes. As an operational objective, liberalism accepts the utilitarian concept of maximizing the happiness of the greatest number of people. The goal is to increase present and future happiness and prosperity for the preponderance of people.

GOVERNMENT'S DUTIES. It is the public sector's primary obligation to protect individuals from external (international) and internal (domestic) restraints on their freedoms, and its secondary obligation is to enhance and guarantee the socioeconomic welfare of the average person.

GOVERNMENT'S SIZE AND POWER. Government should not be so large as to be overbearing and controlling, but needs to have enough power to accomplish its numerous functions and to do good for its citizens.

GOVERNMENT'S JURISDICTION. The broader jurisdictions of government are superior to the narrower jurisdictions of government in accomplishing what needs to be done. So, to get anything worthwhile achieved, national is favored over state, and state over local government.

For some purposes, international governing bodies are preferred over national governance.

PRIORITIES. For the individual, economic equality and economic security are the primary objectives. For society, economic stability in the short run is the primary objective.

RIGHTS AND RESPONSIBILITIES. People have legal, social and economic rights. Society is obligated to protect and enhance these rights

KEY CONCEPTS

Any discussion of liberalism as a philosophy gets one into dealing with six key concepts, all of them quite familiar to us:
- Freedom (Liberty)
- Equality
- Justice (Fairness, Equity)
- Flourishing (Development, Growth)
- Virtue (Character, Competence)
- Duty (Responsibility, Obligation)

The problem we have in discussing these concepts is that they are so interrelated that separating them from each other becomes difficult. As a result, we will discuss freedom and equality together; justice, which divides into legal, social and distributive justices, by itself; and finally flourishing, virtue and duty together.

FREEDOM AND EQUALITY

The ultimate objective of liberalism has not changed over time. It has always been freedom from restraints for individuals. The pursuit and achievement of this ultimate objective gradually but inexorably gave rise to another important goal, namely equality for the individual. Over time, the freedom goal has morphed into the equality goal. This has been a gradual process, but most people, and especially conservatives, now believe that the primary objective of liberalism is economic, social and political equality for the individual. This is not true! The overriding objective is still freedom, and equality is a secondary but very important operational objective, more a means to an end than an end in itself.

The pursuit and achievement of freedom as an ultimate objective has taken place in a series of steps involving different short-term, intermediate, working or operational objectives. When reasonable success has been achieved at any step, liberalism changes its emphasis and moves to the next step with a different intermediate objective. When one working objective is achieved to an acceptable degree, liberalism moves to a different working objective. We find that there have been ten steps or operational objectives. They are presented here in approximate order of their first appearance, but please recognize some limitations:

- The various steps overlap so that we can be in several steps at the same time.
- The length of time involved in any specific step can be quite long. In fact, some of the working objectives have gone out of vogue and then back in favor.
- Dating the various steps would be difficult if not impossible.
- Some analysts would disagree on the order of first appearance of the various short-term goals.

With these limitations in mind, let's look at the ten steps.

STEP ONE: The very first operational objective was freedom from restraints imposed by religion and law. Classical liberalism sought to eliminate both the privileges of the upper classes and restraints on ordinary people imposed by the church and legal system. Ordinary people, and especially the lower classes, were seen as being oppressed by the church and by government. Liberals spoke out against such oppression and in support of the freedoms associated with markets and business. In essence, liberals were allied with business against the church and government. The working objectives were equality in religion and law. The former meant eliminating the special privileges of royalty (the divine right of kings) and the aristocracy (the superior rights of landlords and wealthy land owners). The latter meant getting rid of the shabby treatment of poor people in both legislation and the courts (long periods of incarceration for petty crimes).

STEP TWO: The second operational objective was elimination of the worst abuses of business. Liberals came to see the business community as the primary source of oppression of low-income workers. So liberals turned to government to indirectly help the lower classes by limiting what business could do with its labor force. The result was the development of minimum wages, maximum hours, and child labor laws. In essence, liberals became increasingly allied with government against the business community, not so much small business as the owners of factories.

STEP THREE: The third operational objective was the elimination of extreme poverty. Liberals came to see living conditions in urban industrial communities as unacceptable. They put pressure on the public sector and private charities to help those who were the worst off. This was the start of the welfare system on a very limited basis.

STEP FOUR: The fourth operational objective was the restriction of business power. Liberals saw big business as having too much economic control and the ability to exploit the working classes. So they promoted government regulation of the business sector, antitrust laws to limit monopoly power, and either government ownership or control of public utilities. They also supported the formation of unions as a countervailing power to big business.

STEP FIVE: The fifth operational objective was help for low-income groups. Liberals supported the establishing of public schools to educate young people, both to facilitate their making a decent living when they grew up and to make them better citizens. They also supported government legislation that provided some minimum income for those who lost their livelihood because of sickness, old age, industrial accident or unemployment. This was the beginning of liberal governments trying not only to put a floor under income but also to limit risk for their citizens.

STEP SIX: The sixth operational objective was to seek limits on the accumulation of wealth. Liberals did not mind there being differences in income and wealth between the lower middle classes and the upper middle classes, but they objected to the extreme differences in income and wealth between the upper and lower classes. So they supported inheritance taxes and progressive income taxes.....and the more progressive the better.

STEP SEVEN: The seventh operational objective was to eliminate restraints on individual behavior. Liberals were a major factor in the weakening, many would say destruction, of traditional values and previously accepted limits to behavior.

> The new way of thinking in current times is that anything goes, so long as nobody gets hurt in the process. So we accept everything from body and facial piercing to butt tattoos. In the minds of some of us, the weird has become the norm.

STEP EIGHT: The eighth operational objective was to support excluded groups seeking legal rights and social recognition. Liberals were among the early supporters of civil rights for first women and then ethnic minorities. With victory achieved in these areas, liberals turned to supporting smaller fringe and outcast groups such as gays and illegal immigrants. In essence, liberals allied with government against the existing social order, trying to make society accept what was previously the unacceptable.

STEP NINE: The ninth operational objective was to limit business decisions that directly affect people—workers, customers and society as a whole. The requirement that almost everything must be disclosed to everybody affected has dramatically increased the paperwork and legal burdens of the business community and is especially onerous to small firms. The need to justify every significant hiring and firing decision makes government a major part of the management team.

STEP TEN: The tenth operational objective was to eliminate most risks for most people, making this nation virtually a risk-free society. With liberals leading the way, a vast majority of us have come to accept the social need to insure people from the extreme risks that most of us face, such as the premature death of a family's primary breadwinner or major illnesses and accidents that prevent one from earning a living. But social and private insurance programs have been extended to cover related day-to-day expenses. So medical insurance—both public and private—has gone from coverage of hospitalization and surgeries to paying for an annual checkup at the doctor's office and every inexpensive pill the doctor prescribes. These are everyday expected expenses that one can budget for personally rather than expect society to pay.

Because of liberals, America is becoming the nanny state with government expected to protect its citizens from every economic contingency, even those that are self-inflicted (smoking and drug abuse) and easily prevented (obesity).

THE BOTTOM LINE: When one looks at how liberalism sought individual freedom and equality in America, starting with the colonial era, certain conclusions can be drawn:

- While liberalism started out allied with the business world to limit government power over the individual, it quickly turned to government for help in controlling business.
- Liberalism has right from the beginning sought to help the working class and lower-income groups.
- Freedom was always liberalism's first priority. At first it sought negative freedom—freedom from restraints on individuals by the church, by law, by regulation, and by business. Then it turned to positive freedom—freedom for individuals to make most decisions for themselves and do their own thing without any restraints imposed by inadequate income or social barriers.
- Equality steadily emerged as a major liberal objective, but it also went through stages: equality in the eyes of the church, equality in the law, equality in economic and social opportunity, and finally greater equality in economic and social outcomes.
- In order to achieve more freedom and equality for the lower classes, liberals have been willing to restrain, limit and even pull down the upper classes. They have seemingly found it easier to hold back the small number of rich people rather than provide help to the far larger number of poor people.

JUSTICE

Justice is a complex subject with many nuances attached to its meaning. It is seen as encompassing fairness, equity, righteousness, validity and impartiality. It is the administration of law according to prescribed, accepted and known principles. It is the use of power and authority to uphold what is just, right and lawful. It is the quality of being just and fair.

There are three types of justice:

- **LEGAL JUSTICE**—the proper and unbiased administration of the law, and the fair and equitable treatment of all individuals within the legal system.
- **SOCIAL JUSTICE**—the extension and protection of human rights, equal economic opportunity, personal dignity and fair treatment to all members of society, regardless of sex, age, race, religion and class.
- **DISTRIBUTIVE JUSTICE**—the equitable and proper allocation of economic and social benefits among different people and groups in society.

The early liberals sought legal justice in England and America. The goal was better treatment for the masses—the lower-income groups—in the courts, and the elimination of legal privileges for the social, political, religious and economic aristocracy. After this was sufficiently achieved, the emphasis shifted to social justice. The battles for women's rights and ethnic rights have largely been won, at least in the English-speaking world, but there are continuing concerns for gay rights and immigrant rights. Given what is happening to Muslims in modern society, we may be seeing the reemergence of concerns for religious rights.

The modern emphasis has shifted toward the concept of distributive justice—the proper allocation of goods and benefits among different people, individually or collectively. Theories of distributive justice need to answer these important questions:

- What goods or benefits are to be distributed? The major possibilities are income, wealth, respect, status and power. Note, however, that what is to be distributed could include exemption from some form of negative punishment.
- Among what individuals or groups are these goods or benefits to be distributed? Who makes the list and who doesn't?
- What are the proper criteria for determining how these goods or benefits are to be distributed?

Where do the standards for justice come from? What are their origins? Philosophers talk in terms of only three possibilities:

- **DIVINE REVELATION**. Many religious people believe that the standard for justice, the essence of morality, and the fundamental basis for law all come from God.

- **DISCOVERY OF NATURAL LAW**. All human actions and choices have natural consequences. People get what they deserve or are entitled to—their just deserts—based upon what they do and the decisions they make. This is the essence of natural law. It is true across all societies, no matter how different they are from each other. Thus, natural law is both universal and absolute.
- **HUMAN CREATION**. Most legal systems evolve over time on the basis of human experience with the law and its outcomes.

> One of the major arguments among early liberals was whether justice was derived from divine revelation or natural law. That debate has died out as the modern liberals almost universally believe that justice is a human or social creation.

Distributive justice as defined by human creation can be based on equality, need, contribution, merit or social status. Let's look at each:

EQUALITY. Egalitarians believe that there can be no such thing as distributive justice without social, political, legal and economic equality. Claims of both freedom and justice without equality are meaningless. Equality is justice in this view. However, we need to make three important points about equality in distribution:

- Communism and socialism are socioeconomic systems that support social, political, legal and economic equality, at least in theory. However, neither has been able to achieve income and wealth distributions that are significantly more equal than those in capitalistic systems.
- The main problem with equality relates to incentives for work, effort and innovation. In the long run, the lower classes may be better off if inequality generates incentives that increase society's real output and productivity over time than if current levels of real output are evenly distributed in the short run. In brief, equality may be beneficial immediately but harmful eventually.
- The focus of modern debate relates to strong differences of opinion about equality of opportunity and equality of outcome. As a general

rule, those who are more liberal lean toward equal outcomes and those who are more conservative toward equal opportunities.

NEED. Those who support needs-based theories of justice believe that such basic goods as food, housing, education, medical care and the like should be distributed and guaranteed to all members of society. There are two issues relating to this approach:

- How much of each good should be distributed before incentive problems are created?
- In an advanced society, what goods should be guaranteed to everyone? Don't we all need transportation, television and computers to be able to play a meaningful role in a society such as ours?

CONTRIBUTION. This approach is simply that those who contribute the most to society get the greatest rewards from society. Effort, ability and innovation get paid. This, of course, is the very foundation of a capitalist economic system. It results, if historical experience is a worthwhile guide, in the highest average standard of living. Its drawback is inequality. There can be very wide disparities in income, wealth, economic and political power, and even social status. And such can generate envy and social unrest among those near the bottom of the economic ladder.

MERIT AND SOCIAL STATUS. In reality, this is not a separate way of thinking, but just an adjunct to the contribution approach. It adds to the list those people who are deemed especially deserving even though they don't produce much for society. We might include the community's stars in this category: professional athletes, entertainers, literary writers, and even some politicians.

FLOURISHING, VIRTUE, OBLIGATION

The concepts of flourishing, virtue and obligation are interconnected. In this section, we will define our terms and then look at how the three concepts are connected to each other in liberalism.

FLOURISHING: To flourish is to thrive, prosper and succeed. To flourish is to develop and improve. Using a gardening analogy, flourishing is to flower, bloom or grow. When it comes right down to it, the ultimate objective of liberalism is for the individual to flourish. What is required for that to happen?

- The individual must have options to choose from. This has two implications: first, that society guarantees the freedoms and rights necessary to give the individual the power of choice; and second, that the individual has personal abilities, broadly defined, that make his or her options meaningful.
- The choices made by the individual must involve not only a personally worthwhile objective but also a challenge. What one chooses must be meaningful to the individual; it may not be meaningful to society.

VIRTUE (often thought of as civic virtue): Virtue is showing moral excellence, living one's life according to moral and ethical principles, thus setting a standard for others. It is having a set of particularly effective and beneficial qualities which define our concept of good character (being courageous, wise, just, honest, principled, sincere, humane, prudent, temperate, practical, and excelling in whatever one does.) Civic virtue can be thought of as being dedicated to the overall welfare of the entire community, broadly defined, being willing to make political decisions based not on what is in your own self-interest and your personal beliefs, but rather on what you perceive to be in the best interest for the community as a whole—the common good. To simplify the concept, we can just think of civic virtue as being what we want our politicians, both elected and appointed officeholders, to be like. To me, virtue is the combination of character and competence.

Where does (civic) virtue come from? How do people acquire character and competence? In a free society civic virtue has always come from our families, neighborhoods, churches and synagogues, schools, unions, charitable organizations, social clubs, and voluntary civic associations (the Lions Club and Better Business Bureau). Collectively, these are thought of as society's nongovernmental institutions. Some give us character and competence; others give us experience in dealing with other people of civic virtue. But it is from these nongovernmental institutions that society acquires men and women of virtue—character and competence—that are able and willing to be our leaders.

OBLIGATION: the liberal concept of obligation is really a continuum of three words: obligation, responsibility and duty. Although related, each has a slightly different meaning:

- Obligation is a commitment, what one is bound to do to fulfill a promise or social requirement.
- Responsibility is an obligation to do what you are asked to do, to do something worthwhile, and to do it without supervision. The responsible person is accountable for something, someone else, or him- or herself. The responsible person is expected to distinguish between right and wrong, to act rationally, to be dependable and trustworthy, and to be accountable for his or her own decisions and behavior.
- Duty is a moral commitment to something or someone. Duty is action we commit to without self-interest. Duty is conduct required by one's personal sense of justice and morality, by the dictates of one's own conscience. An individual's sense of duty arises from one's place in society, character, and moral expectations. Duty always shows respect for some ideal. Duty always imposes some cost or burden on the individual. Civic duties are the social obligations of citizens to the state and responsibilities for the protection and improvement of the community.

CONNECTIONS: With definitions in place, the interconnections are fairly obvious. When individuals flourish in a liberal society, they develop virtue—both character and competence. Such virtuous individuals recognize and accept obligations to society. They assume responsibility for themselves and for others. They have civic duties to be fulfilled. Turning these statements around, a liberal society needs people with civic virtue for leadership and involvement. Such individuals will only arise in a society that allows and encourages them to flourish.

LIBERALISM AND DEMOCRACY

Liberal or representative democracy first arose in Europe in the 18th century during the Age of Enlightenment. Until then, most states were monarchies with power held by the monarch or aristocracy. To justify this, it was widely believed that:

- The masses are uneducated and badly informed, and thus should never be granted decision-making power over any important matters.
- People are inherently violent, selfish, corrupt, malicious and evil; they needed strong leadership to control their impulses.

- Democracy would be inherently unstable because the beliefs and desires of the masses would be constantly changing.
- Monarchs ruled by divine right preordained by God. They shared power with the aristocracy and religious leaders who were better educated and informed than the masses.
- The needs of the people were unimportant relative to the power of the state. The collective entity took priority over individuals.

Newly-emerging liberalism turned these beliefs upside-down. The intellectuals of the Enlightenment argued that people were inherently good and would improve over time, especially as they became more educated. They believed that all people are created equal and that political power should not be reserved for an upper class as a part of God's will. They thought that governments should serve the people rather than be served by the people. Finally, they felt that government by the people would be acceptably stable and constructive, although this belief was shaken by the terrible excesses of the French Revolution.

America was founded as a republican democracy. The nation and its government were to be led by an educated and propertied elite. Men of virtue—character and competence—were not only the founders but also the only voters and first leaders. The working class, unpropertied men, women and ethnic minorities were pretty well barred from having any say in how the local communities, the several states, and the nation as a whole were to be run. Such was a fact of life in our early republic. The founding fathers earnestly believed that this was the best way for our society to be governed. However, republican government created three problems—it was exclusive, unresponsive and coercive—that eventually led to its being replaced by something quite different:

EXCLUSIVE. Republican government is exclusive. Society and government are run by a small proportion of the people affected. But liberals believe not only that all men are created equal, but also that everyone should have a major say in whatever affects their personal lives. There was thus both philosophical and political pressure to extend the vote to working-class men, women, ethnic minorities and young people. It was no longer just men of property, character and competence that were running things; everyone had a say. Politics was no longer for the elite, but was the province of the masses.

I wonder whether we can really think that just about anyone can get into politics. Perhaps at the local level, but I question whether they can at the higher levels of government. Money matters in politics. The majority of our Presidents, Senators, Governors and Congressmen are millionaires or close to it. In this sense, modern politics is just as exclusive as the republican politics of the past.

UNRESPONSIVE. Republican government is unresponsive to change. In the beginning, the focus of society's and government's interests was primarily at the local community level, only secondarily at the state level, and very remotely at the federal level. A republican form of government controlled by men of virtue—character and competence—was appropriate for such a society. However, the emergence of corporate capitalism expanded the marketplace so that local communities lost control of their local economies and were forced to compete over broader geographical areas, eventually reaching the national and even international levels. Politics and government followed, albeit sometimes with a long time lag. Issues were no longer discussed at the local level but were handed over to the higher levels of government. A different kind of political leader was now needed, one who was not limited to the local community but could see and react to the big picture. In short, America still needed men of character to be its leaders, but the competences that were now necessary were different—more cosmopolitan, sophisticated and technically proficient.

COERCIVE. Republican government is usually coercive. It is relatively easy for smaller communities to promote the kinds of civic virtues needed for effective government. The number of people involved is small, the community is close knit and there is a commonality of interests. There is a correct way of thinking within the community, and to be an accepted part of society, one must adhere to that way of thinking. Coercion and conformity exist but they are subtle and social in nature. But as the numbers increase, the people become more diverse and different interests appear.

The development of civic virtue is much more difficult. If it is to be maintained, education and training must become more arduous and focused on a correct way of thinking. But this form of coercion is difficult to maintain in a free society with a very diverse population.

As a direct result of the problems with republican democracy, government in the United States has gradually but steadily evolved into what has come to be called a liberal or representative democracy. In an 1863 speech, Abraham Lincoln defined our democracy as "government of the people, by the people, and for the people." Such a democracy is characterized by certain things:

- regular and competitive elections between two (or more) different political parties in which voters—a vast majority of the adult population—have a definite choice;
- a peaceful transition of power as the losers in an election become the loyal opposition, perhaps disagreeing with the policies of the winners but accepting the judgment of the voters and the validity of the democratic process;
- separation of powers and a system of checks and balances among the different parts of government—not only among the federal, state and local levels, but also among the administrative, legislative and judicial branches;
- a pluralistic society in which human rights and civil liberties are established and protected equally for everyone, no matter what their personal characteristics and beliefs;
- an open society in which there is a definite distinction between the state and society, and in which freedom and the rule of law hold sway over every-day life; and
- a strong constitution protecting all of the above and limiting the authority of government.

We tend to take these things for granted in America. If you look around the world, however, you see that they are not common and many countries we think of as democracies do not have all six characteristics.

Liberal or representative democracy, even as practiced in this country, is open to criticism on several interrelated counts:

TYRANNY OF THE MAJORITY: Democracy can allow a majority to limit the rights and take advantage of a minority. Historically, this was clearly the case of the white majority limiting the rights and socioeconomic status of the black minority in this country. Currently, some believe that the majority of lower-income voters wants to take advantage of the much smaller minority of high-income people by instituting very high marginal income tax rates on them.

VOTER INCENTIVES: In most major elections, voters lack incentives to become informed about the issues and candidates or even to vote. This has two undesirable effects: First, a minority with special interests is more likely to get its way. Because the old vote in large numbers and the young do not, this has made such programs as Social Security and Medicare the "third rail of American politics." Second, low voter turnout, no matter whether caused by disenchantment with politics in general or contentment with the way things are, brings into question the legitimacy of election results or even the electoral process itself. It is difficult for an elected official in high office to claim a mandate for his or her programs when only a minority of potential voters supported him or her.

POLITICIAN INCENTIVES: Because of television, the cost of political campaigning has become prohibitive, running into billions for President and many millions for Senator and Governor, even hotly-contested races for Congress. There are three interrelated results: Those with money and willingness to contribute some of it have a lot of influence. Campaigning for the next election begins the day after this election. Politicians shape their views and policies to pander to those who donate. Money talks.

NATURE OF CAMPAIGNING: There are several disturbing aspects of modern political campaigns. They value performance and demagoguery over substance and character. They emphasize sound bites, short and catchy statements that can be repeated over and over again without any elaboration. They emphasize negativity, criticizing the character and past statements of opponents far more than saying anything positive about the candidate's own experience and program.

SHORT-TERM ORIENTATION: The constant drive of politicians to seek reelection gives them a short-term orientation. Policies with benefits up front and costs delayed into the future are favored over those with short-term costs and benefits primarily in the long run. A modern example of the former is the Patient Protection and Affordable Care Act, commonly known as Obamacare. A key example of the latter is most environmental legislation and regulation. What politician will vote for a policy that reduces employment today but improves the environment tomorrow? Another aspect of this short-term orientation is politicians under political pressure to do something, anything to appease voter demands doing something they know to be wrong. This has come to be called "mob rule." The classic historical example is that of Richard Nixon, a conservative Republican under pressure to do something about inflation, instituting wage and price controls in spite of his having past experience with their perverse effects.

There is one more fundamental problem with modern liberal or representative democracy. It may sow the seeds of its own destruction. The basic difficulty is that the more numerous lower classes have the political power to vote themselves benefits that the fewer members of the upper classes cannot and will not pay for. This readily increases over time, causing political unrest among the majority, who turn to more exacting and draconian measures to satisfy their demands on society. The tyranny of the majority becomes more oppressive and dictatorial. The situation is ripe for the emergence of one-party rule and even autocracy. The fundamentals of democracy disappear.

Ancient Rome once was a democracy ruled by its senate, but it turned to emperors who provided bread and circuses to the masses. Argentina was the third richest country per capita in the world (behind the US and UK) only to have its working classes fall under the spell of Juan Peron and thus to plummet to becoming a second-tier nation. When one sees the social and economic decline of much of Europe and its welfare state, one must wonder about its future. Many people see America following in Europe's footsteps.

Why? My view is that the evolution of our democracy from the republican to the liberal version is the crux of the problem. Too many people have the right to vote. We have gone from the situation at our nation's founding when an educated and propertied elite had the vote to the current circumstances in which almost everyone can vote. We have gone too far. Nobody argues that working-class men, women, and ethnic minorities should not have the right to vote. But we can ask such questions as these: Should one have to be proficient in the English language to vote? Should one have at least a high school education or equivalent to vote? Should one have to be at least twenty-one to vote?

In my view, in the short run we should all be treated as equals with the same rights and liberties. We are not all equal, however, in our ability to determine the long-run future of our nation. Where we should draw the line is a difficult question, but whether we should draw a line, in my opinion, is not. Liberalism has a tendency to go too far; liberal democracy has the same inclination.

But never forget the words of Winston Churchill, England's Prime Minister, when he told the House of Commons that: "Nobody pretends that democracy is perfect or all-wise. Indeed, it has been said that democracy is the worst form of government except for all other forms that have been tried from time to time."[2]

DISSENT

Liberalism is the philosophy of dissent, of seeking change in established policies, of opposition to entrenched power. It can vary in significance from the most minor disagreement over a single decision made by a local organization with few members to a political upheaval by millions against a government that has been repressive of its people for decades. It can cover a wide range of activities from simple protest demonstrations to violent revolutions involving military force. And it can involve known liberals, such as gays seeking marital rights, or groups that are anything but liberal, such as conservatives objecting to abortion. No matter who is involved, dissent is a liberal process.

In theory, there are only three levels of dissent. What is interesting about them is the different reactions to each by liberals and conservatives. The three forms of dissent are as follows:

PEACEFUL PROTEST WITHIN THE LAW. Here we are talking about such things as peaceful demonstrations and protest marches seeking to get a point across to the general public, some governmental body or even a major corporation. By and large, liberals are sympathetic towards peaceful protest, conservatives less so, although the Tea Party definitely moved toward using various forms of public protest within the law.

PEACEFUL PROTEST OUTSIDE THE LAW. Here we are talking about crossing a line so that some aspect of law is broken. People get arrested for minor offenses; here in America, it's usually for trespassing or resisting arrest. Punishments are usually minor—small fines or a night in jail. Such punishment is expected and accepted by the perpetrators. Liberals are lenient toward those engaged in this type of civil disobedience, conservatives again less so because they usually believe in fairly strict adherence to the law.

VIOLENT PROTEST WELL OUTSIDE THE LAW. Here we are talking about the violent forms of protest fueled by anger and frustration over what are seen to be major injustices. Most of us strongly oppose the use of fire-bombings, assault of police officers, the murder of those who do things that offend others (such as abortion doctors), and the like. However, note two things: First, we have all heard, when violent forms of protest take place, someone say that they understand the frustration and motives of those who resort to violence when the protest involved is about something the commentator agrees with. And that is true on both sides of the political spectrum. Second, Americans almost always oppose violent protest when it occurs inside America or other democratic countries, but they generally support violent protest and armed revolution against the governments of autocratic nations. This is consistent with the liberal philosophy that people have the right to use force to change either the form or leadership of government when they perceive that their fundamental rights are being denied.

The bottom line is that dissent is a liberal process, no matter whether it is used by those on the political left or right. However, social acceptance is always a matter of degree and viewpoint.

MODERATE AND EXTREME LIBERALS

When one examines the sweep of modern American history, one is struck by the tendency for our Democratic presidents to roughly alternate between being moderate liberals and extreme or radical liberals. Roosevelt was elected as a moderate but became much more radical in changing the fundamental nature of our society and economy through the New Deal. Truman and Kennedy were moderates, although Kennedy moved American society away from racism. Johnson was again more radical in changing our society and economy through all the programs of his Great Society. Both Carter and Clinton were moderates. Obama is generally regarded as being radically or extremely liberal because of his approaches to fiscal budgets, foreign policy, government regulation and medical care. What all this shows is that liberalism moves forward through time in a process of fits and starts, rapid change and consolidation (with the latter occurring under both moderate Democrat and Republican presidents).

FOOTNOTES
1. Alan Wolfe; "The Future of Liberalism;" Alfred A. Knopf; 2009
2. Winston Churchill; speech to the House of Commons; 11/11/1947

5

CONSERVATISM

In 1860, when asked what conservatism was, Abraham Lincoln responded, "Is it not adherence to the old and tried, against the new and untried?" While simplistic, that's actually a pretty good definition. Let's look at some alternatives possibilities:

- Conservatism is a social philosophy that supports the maintenance of and only gradual change in traditional customs and institutions.
- Conservatism is an economic philosophy that supports free markets, small government, low taxes and limited regulation of economic activity.
- Conservatism is a political philosophy that opposes the basic principles and policies of communism, socialism and liberalism. (In many ways it is a negative rather than a positive movement.)

Modern conservatism is a heterogeneous movement. It can be thought of as having at least five branches, each emphasizing somewhat different aspects of conservatism:

SOCIAL (TRADITIONAL) CONSERVATISM supports traditional values, customs and institutions, primarily in the belief that society benefits from continuity with the past and suffers from rapid and revolutionary change.

RELIGIOUS CONSERVATISM supports traditional values, customs and institutions, but primarily for moral and religious reasons.

ECONOMIC CONSERVATISM supports free markets, private property, strong incentives, a small public sector, low tax rates and limited government regulation of economic activity.

Economic conservatism covers a wide range of beliefs. As pointed out in the first chapter, there can be marked differences between big business managers (CEOs and CFOs), entrepreneurs, and those who are policy-oriented.

LIBERTARIAN CONSERVATISM also supports free markets, private property, strong incentives, a small public sector, low tax rates and limited government regulation of economic activity, but seeks a very limited role for government and societal norms in social relationships as well.

NEOCONSERVATISM supports nationalism, expanding America's influence around the world, and spreading American-style economic and political systems. It is less hostile to big government than other types of conservatism.

One cannot discuss conservatism as a movement without considering the role talk radio and talk television play in marshaling conservative forces. Rush Limbaugh, Sean Hannity, Glenn Beck, Michael Savage, Mark Levin and others have all contributed to conservatism by attracting many new believers and bringing conservative beliefs and issues to the public's attention.

EDMUND BURKE (1729-1797)

Edmund Burke served for three decades in the British House of Commons and was one of the most influential members of Parliament. He is best remembered for his support for the American Revolution and opposition to the French Revolution. He is generally thought to be the founding father of and philosophical inspiration for modern conservatism, a long way ahead of his time.

Burke believed that the American colonies had justifiable grievances against the government of King George III. He thought of the Revolutionary War as a civil war fought between Englishmen at home and Englishmen in the Colonies. He saw the irony of a Germanic King using German mercenaries to crush the English liberties of English colonists. He had mixed feelings about the American Revolution, opposing oppression and injustice, but fearing the loss of the richest jewel of the British Empire.

While Burke supported the American Revolution, he opposed and feared the French Revolution, and especially the danger of its spreading throughout Europe and possibly even into democratic England itself. His case against having what was happening in France sweep the continent can be summarized as follows:

- The French Revolution was excessively violent. The monarchy and much of the aristocracy was killed off, as was a significant part of the middle classes and even some of the revolutionary movement's own leaders. Fearing death and imprisonment, many good people fled France.
- The French Revolution effectively destroyed the social, political and economic fabric of France. All ties with the past were gone. Everything had to be rebuilt from the ground up.
- The French Revolution sought to give rise to a democracy of the lower classes that were unfit and unprepared for governance. It was mob rule—tyrannical and bloody with no room for dissent.
- The French Revolution curtailed for all time the role of religion and the Roman Catholic Church in France with a major loss of moral inspiration and leadership.
- The French Revolution was based on a belief the government could be used to remake and improve human nature, something deemed to be impossible by conservatives who see man as inherently selfish and even evil.

It should be noted that there were many who wanted to have a democracy of the lower classes in England. Burke led the political fight against this. It is a tribute to him and his leadership that there never was a British Revolution like what took place in France.

Burke did not believe in a democracy in which virtually everyone had a vote. He opposed such a democracy because:

- good government requires levels of intelligence and knowledge greater than those of the uninformed common people;
- the common people all too often have unstable and heated passions that could be turned by demagogues against even the most beneficial of society's traditions and institutions; and
- the masses would too often oppress unpopular minorities in a tyranny of the majority.

For these reasons, Edmund Burke favored a government of the educated and propertied upper classes, what we call republican democracy.

Burke, however, supported the principles of representative government. He believed that a legislator owes allegiance to the interests and opinions of his constituents, and should put their interests ahead of his own. It is his duty and responsibility, however, to always favor his own mature judgment of his constituents' best long-term interests over their short-term opinions.

Finally, Burke believed that a good society gradually evolved out of the past. It started with religious law or natural law coming to us through divine revelation or reflection on the very nature of mankind. Prescription was the foundation for social order. Society's long-standing customs, traditions and institutions moderated human behavior. They have continued to exist for many generations for good reason, namely that they incorporate and assimilate society's collective wisdom. In short, Burke did not dream of a utopian future but was nostalgic for the past.

RUSSELL KIRK (1918-1994)

Russell Kirk was the ideological inspiration for conservatism in America. His great book, The Conservative Mind, was published in 1953 and is widely read to this day. It defined conservatism as:

- the preservation of long-standing moral customs and tradition;
- respect for the wisdom of our ancestors;
- belief that society is a living and spiritual reality; and
- a willingness to accept gradual and evolutionary social adjustment but a reluctance to allow rapid and revolutionary change.

Kirk is best known for having enumerated six fundamental canons of conservative belief in the opening chapter of The Conservative Mind. They can be interpreted as follows:

1. **Belief in a transcendent order or consummate body of natural law that governs both society as a whole and individual conscience.** This unchanging standard comes from and is based on divine revelation, natural law and/or tradition. There are such things as right and wrong, truth and falsehood. Moral standards are absolute and unchanging, not relative and modified to fit society. At their core, political problems are religious and moral problems.

2. **Devotion to and acceptance of a wide variety of different lifestyles.** This implies opposition to the uniformity and egalitarianism of liberal and radical socioeconomic systems. Difference is accepted, but sameness is not.

3. **Belief that civilized society requires social, political and economic inequality and classes.** People are only equal before God and in the law; otherwise, they are naturally different from each other, both physically and mentally. An upper class is required to provide leadership in society. There can be no such thing as a "classless" community.

4. **Belief that to be free people must be able to own and control private property.** An inseparable link exists between property and liberty. The redistribution of wealth through taxation and other forms of economic leveling does not improve society.

5. **Faith in the lessons of history, custom and tradition.** Things are the way they are for a reason. Customs and traditions that have stood the test of time are passed down from generation to generation and put a limit on human misbehavior, both individual and collective.

6. **Recognition that social innovation and reform cannot deviate too far from existing social customs and traditions.** Change for the sake of change is not progress. To be worthwhile, change must be slow and evolutionary, not rapid and revolutionary.

Kirk was extremely critical of liberals and other left-wing radicals. We can highlight his litany of complaints against them in his following descriptions, all of which he vehemently rejected:

- The left believes in the ultimate perfectibility of man and possibility of steady improvement of society over time. It believes that a combination of education, sound public policies and providing the correct social environment are the keys to a better future. It rejects the conservative notion that man is "fallen"—by nature sinful and violent.

- The left holds religion, custom and tradition in contempt. It is reason that guides the left. Utopian dreams of the future are more important for the left than historical lessons of the past in determining the course of human history.

- The left seeks egalitarian outcomes. It seeks social, political and economic leveling. Class distinctions, the privileges of aristocracy, and differences in income and wealth are all to be eliminated in a new social order.

- The left favors rapid and revolutionary social change through central government, usually based on utopian concepts of a better life.

Russell Kirk was optimistic about the future of conservatism, and believed that, although often defeated and weakened, it would endure in America because it was built on four firm foundations that have remained intact:

- The United States remains a bastion of religious and especially Christian belief, more so than any other western nation.
- The Constitution of the United States, probably the most powerful conservative public document ever written, is still in place and, although all too often liberally interpreted, has stood the test of time for well over two centuries.
- The American concept of the separation of powers among the three branches of government, and between federal, state and local levels of government, has worked well and diffused political power convincingly.
- Private property and the right to it have remained one of the most accepted institutions in America.

In his many books and columns, Russell Kirk often discussed what conservatives need to do not only to be politically attractive to the voters but also to make America a better place to live. Several themes appear in these writings:

- Conservatives must promote spiritual renewal and a return to religion, not just for themselves but for society as a whole. Faith and the development of character provide a solid foundation for leading a good and satisfactory life.
- Conservatives must help society develop leadership abilities. This requires both the acquisition of leadership skills through experience in civil institutions and the provision of a solid, fundamental education to everyone.
- Conservatives must openly resist the political ideologies of the liberal left. Communism and socialism are the antithesis of conservatism, but all utopian schemes are suspect and inimical to the best long-term interests of the common people, no matter how alluring they seem in theory. Of particular importance is avoiding schemes for the redistribution of income and wealth which, although attractive in the short run, are not in the best interests of the lower classes in the long run.

- Conservatives must seek ways to help the masses—the lower classes—attain personal satisfaction with their present lives, a sense of belonging, and hope for the future. Obligations and duties should come before rights and interests, because their fulfillment usually adds considerably to personal gratification.

- Conservatives must develop society's sense of true community through the strengthening of the family, voluntary institutions, and lower levels of government. Roots and a commonality of interests must be used to overcome the problems of diversity and rapid change that isolate and harm too many individuals.

Late in life Russell Kirk wrote one more great book, "The Politics of Prudence."[1] In it he presented a summary of conservative assumptions—ten articles of belief—that differed somewhat from his six canons of "The Conservative Mind." In my opinion, this is the clearest statement of modern American conservative thought ever written and it is a shame that it has been so ignored. Even though we have devoted considerable space already to Russell Kirk, it is certainly worthwhile to include his final statement of what conservatism is all about. Using his own words, here is an abridged version of his ten articles of belief:

First, the conservative believes that there exists an enduring moral order. Moral truths are permanent. Order signifies harmony. A society in which men and women are governed by belief in an enduring moral order, by a strong sense of right and wrong, by personal convictions about justice and honor, will be a good society—whatever political machinery it may utilize; while a society in which men and women are morally adrift, ignorant of norms, and intent chiefly upon gratification of appetites, will be a bad society—no matter how liberal its formal constitution may be.

Second, the conservative adheres to custom, convention, and continuity. It is old custom that enables people to live together peaceably. Continuity is the means of linking generation to generation; it matters as much for society as it does for the individual; without it, life is meaningless. Order and justice and freedom are the artificial products of a long social experience, the result of centuries of trial and reflection and sacrifice. Necessary change ought to be gradual and discriminatory, never unfixing old interests at once.

Third, conservatives believe in the principle of prescription—that is, all things established by immemorial usage. We are unlikely to make any brave new discoveries in morals or politics or tastes. The individual is foolish, but the species is wise. The human race has acquired a prescriptive wisdom far greater than any man's petty private rationality.

Fourth, conservatives are guided by their principle of prudence. In the statesman, prudence is chief among virtues. Any public measure ought to be judged by its probable long-run consequences, not merely by temporary advantage or popularity. Liberals and radicals are imprudent, for they dash at their objectives without giving much heed to the risk of new abuses worse than the evils they hope to sweep away. Human society being complex, remedies cannot be simple if they are to be efficacious. The conservative acts only after sufficient reflection, having weighed the consequences.

Fifth, conservatives pay attention to the principle of variety. They feel affection for the proliferating intricacy of long-established social institutions and modes of life, as distinguished from the narrowing uniformity and deadening egalitarianism of radical systems. For the preservation of a healthy diversity in any civilization, there must survive orders and classes, differences in material condition, and many sorts of inequality. The only true forms of equality are equality at the Last Judgment and equality before a just court of law; all other attempts at leveling must lead, at best, to social stagnation.

Sixth, conservatives are chastened by their principal of imperfectability. Human nature suffers irremediably from certain grave faults. Man being imperfect, no perfect social order ever can be created. To seek for utopia is to end in disaster. All that we reasonably can expect is a tolerably ordered, just, and free society, in which some evils, maladjustments, and suffering will continue to lurk. By proper attention to prudent reform, we may preserve and improve this tolerable order. But if the old institutional and moral safeguards of a nation are neglected, then the anarchic impulse in humankind breaks loose.

Seventh, conservatives are persuaded that freedom and property are closely linked. Separate property from private possession, and Leviathan becomes master of all. Upon the foundation of private property, great civilizations are built. The more widespread is the possession of private property, the more stable and productive is a commonwealth. Economic leveling is not economic progress. The institution of private property has been a powerful instrument for teaching men and women responsibility, for providing motives to integrity, for supporting general culture, for raising mankind above the level of mere drudgery, for affording leisure to think and freedom to act. To be able to retain the fruits of one's labor; to be able to see one's work made permanent; to be able to bequeath one's property to one's posterity; to be able to rise from the natural condition of grinding poverty to the security of enduring accomplishment; to have something that is really one's own—these are advantages difficult to deny. The conservative acknowledges that the possession of property fixes certain duties upon the possessor; he accepts those moral and legal obligations cheerfully.

Eighth, conservatives uphold voluntary community, quite as they oppose involuntary collectivism. Although Americans have been attached strongly to privacy and private rights, they also have been a people conspicuous for a successful spirit of community. In a genuine community, the decisions most directly affecting the lives of citizens are made locally and voluntarily. Some of these functions are carried out by local political parties, others by private associations: so long as they are kept local and are marked by the general agreement of those affected, they constitute healthy community. But when these functions pass to centralized authority, then community is in serious danger. If the functions of community are transferred to distant political direction, real government by the consent of the governed gives way to a standardizing process hostile to freedom and human dignity. A nation is no stronger than the numerous little communities of which it is composed. A central administration, or a core of select managers and civil service, however well intentioned and well trained, cannot confer justice and prosperity and tranquility upon a mass of men and women deprived of their old responsibilities. It is the performance of our duties in community that teaches us prudence and efficiency and charity.

Ninth, the conservative perceives the need for prudent restraints upon power and upon human passions. A state in which an individual or a small group is able to dominate the wills of their fellows without check is a despotism. The conservative endeavors to so limit and balance political power that anarchy or tyranny may not arise. Constitutional restrictions, political checks and balances, adequate enforcement of the laws, the old intricate web of restraints upon will and appetite—these the conservative approves as instruments of freedom and order. A just government maintains a healthy tension between the claims of authority and the claims of liberty.

Tenth, the conservative understands that permanence and change must be recognized and reconciled in a vigorous society. The conservative is not opposed to social improvement. Any healthy society is influenced by two forces: its permanence and its progression. The permanence of the society is formed by those enduring interests and convictions that give us stability and continuity. The progression in a society is that spirit and that body of talents which urge us on to prudent reform and improvement. The liberal and the radical would endanger the heritage bequeathed to us, in an endeavor to hurry us into some dubious paradise. The conservative favors reasoned and temperate progress; he is opposed to the cult of progress, whose votaries believe that everything new necessarily is superior to everything old. Just how much changes society requires, and what sort of change, depend upon the circumstances of an age and a nation.

RELIGION AND CONSERVATISM

On average, conservatives are more religious than liberals. However, not all conservatives are religious and not all religious people are conservatives. The religious right is identified with conservatism, and along with libertarians, is generally thought to be at the more doctrinaire end of the conservative spectrum.

Most but not all religious conservatives believe certain things about God and religion:

- We believe that God exists.
- We believe that God created this world and the universe. This is not necessarily to say that the world was made in our measure of six days, but that it reveals a sophistication too great to leave God out of the process of creation.
- We believe that the great written works of religious faith—the New Testament, the Old Testament—are either the Word of God or at least

divinely inspired and that certain passages, the Ten Commandments for example, are without doubt the definitive Word of God.

- We believe that God's written word is both authoritative and instructional for how people should live their lives.
- We believe that our acceptance of and obedience to the written word of God benefits not only ourselves but also our families, our communities, our nation and even all of humanity. Most particularly, it affects how we see ourselves and our role in life.
- We believe that there is an afterlife, that we are judged, and that there is a Heaven and a Hell. We may have difficulty comprehending what they are like, but we do believe that Heaven and Hell exist.

There is a continuum of belief about God's involvement in the affairs of mankind. Some believe that God is intimately involved on a day-to-day basis in all human activity. Others accept the watchmaker thesis that God brought this world and humanity into existence like an intricate watch, started it ticking, and then let it run without further assistance or interference. A common middle position holds that God continues to undergird and support what he has created, relates to those who call upon Him, and occasionally intervenes in our behalf.

How we view the world is determined by our belief system. If we believe in God and try to follow His instructions, we tend to believe in the absolute and unchanging nature of morality and society's rules and laws. If we don't believe in God, we tend to believe that society's morality, rules and laws are more flexible and can be adjusted to the needs of each society. This is one of the great debates in modern society, absolutism (the conservative position) versus relativism (the liberal position).

One of the most difficult problems with American politics is that Republican conservatives and Democratic liberals are unyielding on many political issues, especially those relating to values, culture, and social questions. It is very difficult for both libertarians and members of the religious right to compromise on positions they hold so fervently. Both groups are seen by many as extremists with radical political positions so hardened that negotiation and even discussion on many issues becomes impossible. The situation has gotten so rigid and uncompromising in the Republican Party that officeholders and candidates, especially at the federal level, have been forced to sign pledges in order to get support; and some well-known moderate Republican politicians have been defeated not by more liberal Democrats in the general election but by more extreme conservative Republicans in the primaries.

We should ask the question: What is the relationship between conservatism, religion, society and governance? We can offer no definitive answer, but a few comments are in order:

- The Founding Fathers clearly expected religion and the church to play an important role in America's future development. The founding documents sought to guarantee the individual's free exercise of religion, while avoiding a monopoly in belief through the formation of a state religion, thus protecting our citizens from religious oppression.

- The Judeo-Christian tradition promotes freedom, virtue, justice and order. Thus, it has been a positive influence on American society and its governance.

- Many liberals are hostile to religion and believe that the state should adopt an anti-religion position. This idea has taken the form of hostility to public displays of religious beliefs and symbols, and even government regulation of religious organizations. This has gone as far as rejection of any display of the Ten Commandments or religious Christmas decorations.

- Other liberals have been quite willing to accept religion when it conforms to their own liberal beliefs and advances their liberal cause. Hence, for example, they welcome religious people whose message supports our responsibility to our physical environment, but argue against a religious message that supports our responsibility for our moral environment. They approve of religion as long as it endorses their view, but object when it attempts to influence their behavior.

- Historically, many of our best conservative philosophers and political leaders took religion, and especially Christianity, seriously as an important institution, but not necessarily as a body of dogma to set the future course for society.

- A majority of conservatives use their religious faith as a guiding principle for personal behavior, but they recognize it as being highly personal and thus try to keep it out of any political discussion. To practice their faith publicly is socially acceptable; to try to convert and recruit others in public is not.

- Many conservatives believe that man is by his nature religious. They thus believe that by rejecting religion, many liberals also reject a fundamental part of human nature. By establishing a state which is not religious, they seek to create a new and different human nature. By rejecting one social institution (religion), they seek to establish a substitute institution (atheism). The problem is that atheism doesn't do what religion does, to inculcate in citizens the virtues of character and competence that society needs. It would be far better for the state to support religion because it does a good job for society.

To close our discussion of religion and conservatism, let's look at something from the internet. It has most recently been called "A Prayer for Our Nation" by Rev. Billy Graham. Before that, it was known as "Paul Harvey's On Air Prayer." It was originally written in 1995 by Bob Russell for the Kentucky Governor's Prayer Breakfast in Frankfort, Kentucky. However, it is best known as "The Prayer of Repentance" delivered by Rev. Joe Wright, Senior Pastor of the Central Christian Church in Wichita, Kansas as the opening prayer at a session of the Kansas House of Representatives in January, 1996. We'll drop the opening and closing in order to look at the heart of the prayer, which provides a pretty good view of how religious conservatives think about a wide range of issues:

- We have lost our spiritual equilibrium and inverted our values.
- We have ridiculed the absolute truth of your Word and called it moral pluralism.
- We have worshiped other gods and called it multiculturalism.
- We have endorsed perversion and called it an alternative lifestyle.
- We have exploited the poor and called it the lottery.
- We have neglected the needy and called it self-preservation.
- We have rewarded laziness and called it welfare.
- We have killed our unborn and called it choice.
- We have shot abortionists and called it justifiable.
- We have neglected to discipline our children and called it building esteem.
- We have abused power and called it political savvy.
- We have coveted our neighbors' possessions and called it ambition.
- We have polluted the air with profanity and pornography and called it freedom of expression.
- We have ridiculed the time-honored values of our forefathers and called it enlightenment.
  With this list, we can just add "Amen."

THE CULTURE OF CONTENTMENT

John Kenneth Galbraith (1908-2006) was one of America's most prolific and acclaimed liberal economists. His popular books were written for a general audience and not economists. For our purposes, one of his last books, "The Culture of Contentment"[2] is of great interest for the understanding of American conservatism. What follows is the essence of his argument.

In modern democratic and capitalist countries like ours, there is a large middle-class that is essentially content with its lot in life and effectively controls political decision-making, no matter what political party is in office. In effect, the affluent constitute Galbraith's culture of contentment. They believe that their higher incomes and greater wealth are well deserved and the result of personal effort, intelligence and virtue. Since they believe that what they have and enjoy is a reward for merit, they can see no acceptable social justification for government action to take it away from them. In their thinking, both the role of government and the level of taxation are to be kept as small as possible. There are, however, three major exceptions:

- government expenditures that provide income to the middle and upper classes, such as Social Security, medical care for the old and farm price supports;
- exemptions and allowances that reduce taxes on the middle and upper classes, such as mortgage interest deductions and lower tax rates on capital gains; and
- expenditures that can be seen as protection for the middle and upper class, such as national defense, fire and police departments, and federal insurance on bank deposits.

This category includes the implicit public commitment that allows no very large financial institutions or other giant corporations to fail. This is why in the financial crisis of 2008 the federal government bailed out a wide range of financial institutions and two of our three major automobile manufacturers with wide political support from both Republicans and Democrats. After all, it is in such large enterprises that the contented majority keeps its money and invests its capital.

In contrast, government expenditures for the benefit of lower income groups are to be kept to a minimum. This accounts for conservative and middle-class opposition to welfare, medical care for the poor, public housing and even public education.

There are some interesting policy implications of Galbraith's culture of contentment and they are directly related to how conservatives and the Republican Party respond to specific policy issues. Some of these are pretty obvious; others are not. An example of the obvious is that the lower classes are necessary to do the kinds of work that the middle and upper classes will not do. There must be a ready supply of workers available for low-wage jobs. This accounts for the fact that conservatives and the Republican Party don't put much effort into preventing illegal immigration from Mexico and Latin America. (It should be pointed out that neither do liberals and the Democratic Party, but the reasons are quite different. They expect to gain political supporters when immigrants, legal or illegal, ultimately become citizens.)

Also obvious is middle-class acceptance of vast inequalities in the distribution of income and wealth. The immense wealth and high income of people like Bill Gates and Warren Buffett are okay. The price of preventing social reductions in one's own income and wealth is willingness to accept far greater amounts for the very rich. To advocate income and wealth redistribution for the upper classes would open up the possibility of similar redistribution for the middle classes. In essence, the contented middle class supports the upper class in order to protect itself from the lower classes.

Far less obvious is the fact that fiscal policy is rarely used to stabilize the economy, especially when it requires higher taxes or lower expenditures to prevent inflation. (Of course, when the economy tanked after the financial crisis of 2008, taxes could be reduced and expenditures increased without too much resistance from the contented majority. After all, it was their economic position that was most threatened. Note, however, that most of the changes benefited the middle and upper classes much more than the lower income groups.) Anyway, it has fallen on monetary policy—the manipulation of the money supply and interest rates—far more than fiscal policy to stabilize the American economy.

THE POSTULATES OF CONSERVATISM

Our discussion of modern conservatism so far has touched upon various fundamental principles that are the very foundation of conservatism. I call such ideas and beliefs postulates because to the vast majority of conservatives they are self-evident and require no proof. What follows is my personal attempt to enumerate most of the postulates of modern conservatism, being as precise as possible in order to avoid confusion and ambiguity as to what most conservatives believe. There are thirteen postulates, each given a descriptive title. There are also a dozen very different postulates of liberalism discussed in the previous chapter. The thirteenth has nothing similar to it in liberal thinking.

HUMAN NATURE. People are flawed. They are selfish, violent, dishonest, lazy and vain. Mankind has not improved in this regard over the millennia. To believe that human nature can be improved through education and law is presumptuous. Man is not perfectible. Progress and reform are slow processes. There can never be a utopia with perfect behavior in a perfect society.

SOCIETY'S RATIONALITY. Society's long-standing customs, traditions and institutions have great value. They are passed down from generation to generation for good reason. They connect the past to the present and the future. They incorporate and assimilate society's collective wisdom, the lessons of history. They moderate human behavior and prevent wrongdoing by both individuals and society as a whole.

MORALITY. Moral standards are absolute and unchanging. They are applicable to both individuals and society as a whole. They are not relative and modifiable to fit different societal circumstances. They are derived from divine revelation, natural law and/or tradition.

CHANGE. Any change in society's customs, institutions and policies should be gradual and evolutionary. Change that is a rapid and revolutionary is not only difficult for people and society to assimilate, but also prone to having unforeseen consequences and creating more problems than it solves.

CAPITALISM. Capitalism based on free markets, private property, private enterprise and competition is the best economic system. It results in higher standards of living and more personal freedom.

INEQUALITY. In a free market economy, inequality in the distribution of income and wealth is required to achieve good economic performance. There are two reasons:

- Differences in income are needed to provide incentives for people to educate themselves, work hard, save more, and invest their savings for productive purposes. This is the path not only to increased personal income but also to the development of many small businesses.
- Differences in wealth are needed to facilitate the development of a relatively rich upper class of people willing to undertake risk and become entrepreneurs, creating larger enterprises in pursuit of profits that can be and usually are reinvested.

DEMOCRACY. Representative democracy is better than direct or plebiscitary democracy. Representation is better at developing reasoned debate, at protecting the rights of unpopular minorities, and at avoiding a tyranny of the majority. Republican democracy with the leadership of a propertied and intellectual elite is best for all of society in the long run.

GOVERNMENT'S DUTIES. It is the public sector's primary obligation to protect individuals from external (international) and internal (domestic) restraints on their freedoms, and its secondary obligation is to enable the individual to pursue his or her own self-interest and socioeconomic welfare.

GOVERNMENT'S SIZE AND POWER. Small and limited government is better than big and powerful government. The roles and functions of government should be circumscribed and enumerated. The diffusion of power, checks and balances, and separation of powers enumerated in the Constitution of the United States are useful methods of limiting government.

GOVERNMENT'S JURISDICTION. Policy formulated and administered by the lower levels of government is better than that by the higher levels of government. It is more readily adaptable to differences in local conditions. It allows for greater experimentation to discover better policies and better methods of administration that can be used by a wide range of governments. Thus, local is preferred to state government, state to national government, and national to international government.

PRIORITIES. For the individual, economic freedom should be given higher priority than economic equality and economic security. For society, economic growth in the long run should be given higher priority than economic stability in the short run. The former are better objectives not only for the upper and middle classes but also for society as a whole in the long run. The latter only seem to be better goals for the lower classes in the short run.

RIGHTS AND RESPONSIBILITIES. The duties, responsibilities and obligations of individuals and groups should be given higher priority than their privileges, benefits and rights. People are better off when they contribute to society than when they receive from society.

MORALITY AND ECONOMICS. There is a positive correlation between good morals and good economics. Such moral values as truth and honesty, the value of work, respect for other people, respect for the property rights of others, and self-control contribute significantly to economic productivity. Many think of this in terms of the Protestant work ethic, but it is endemic to most religions and moral traditions, and especially the Protestant, Catholic and Jewish religions that have historically dominated belief in this country.

Many people worry that moral decline in the United States will directly result in economic atrophy, similar to that which befell the Roman Empire. The various Roman emperors increasingly resorted to force, handouts and public entertainment to keep the rabble masses under control. It was all to no avail. The empire failed far more from internal collapse than from external forces. We can only conclude that moral decline will inevitably lead to social, political, economic and military decline. And we cannot help but wonder whether or not this is the fate of America.

FOOTNOTES
1. Russell Kirk; "The Politics of Prudence"; Intercollegiate Studies Institute; 1993; Chapter 2
2. John Kenneth Galbraith; "The Culture of Contentment"; Houghton Mifflin; 1992

6

FOREIGN POLICY

We have already seen how conservatives and liberals differ in their approaches to domestic economic and social policies. These differences carry over into foreign policy. We can call the one approach conservative realism, the other liberal idealism or liberal internationalism (two alternative names for the same policy). But note two truths about American foreign policy and its close relative—national defense:

First, most Americans know little about our foreign policy and frankly don't care. They look inward and not outward. They would have trouble locating most of the countries that we are most concerned about on a map. Foreign policy becomes an issue only when there is a crisis of some sort, and then two things happen:

- People overwhelming back the President and trust him to do the right thing.
- People want something done about the problem, even if the best course of action is to do nothing, putting political pressure on Washington to act and solve the difficulty immediately.

Second, on domestic issues, most conservatives think alike and most liberals think alike. There are few ideological differences, although subgroups can differ on specific issues. On foreign policy, there is a much wider array of differences. There are those who are conservative on domestic matters but liberal internationalists on foreign policy issues. Likewise, there are those who are liberals on domestic matters but conservative realists on foreign policy issues. The result is that there is usually bipartisan support for our foreign policy with many Republicans backing Democratic presidents and many Democrats backing Republican presidents. Disagreements between the political parties are smaller on foreign policy and national defense than they are on domestic issues and policies.

Before we get into a discussion of the differences between liberals and conservatives in the area of foreign policy and national defense, let's look at the history of our policies since World War I, the foreign-policy problems we currently face, some facts about national defense, and the facts about terrorism.

A BRIEF HISTORY OF FOREIGN POLICY

In the 20th century prior to World War I (1914-1918), American foreign policy could be summed up as a combination of four things:
- isolationism—staying out of European affairs if possible;
- protecting American interests in Asia;
- domination of Latin America; and
- projecting American power through our naval forces.

President Woodrow Wilson tried to keep the US out of World War I but found this to be impossible when Germany began attacking American merchant ships and threatened to seize control of the European continent. Wilson was very reluctant to have America enter the fight, but the reality was that America could not permit any military power to control all or most of Europe. The US at first just supported Britain and France by using its vast industrial capacity to supply the allies with war materials, but eventually deployed troops to help defeat Germany and end the war.

President Wilson was a liberal in temperament, and as such saw the US as defending the moral principle that any country should be able to determine its own destiny. For him, "the war to end wars" had been fought "to make the world safe for democracy." He was instrumental in forming the League of Nations. It was to be an international institution of global governance and collective security designed to replace conflict with negotiation and ensure peaceful resolution of disputes between nations. Unfortunately, a conservative Senate refused to have America join the League of Nations, partly out of political hostility toward the President, but mainly out of a fear that America could be dragged into foreign wars. This was the beginning of two decades of American conservative isolationism.

The 1930s brought America the Great Depression and the election of President Franklin Delano Roosevelt (FDR) for four terms. (When he died in 1945, Harry Truman filled out FDR's last term before winning another term for himself.) American isolationism took an economic form with extraordinarily high tariffs imposed on foreign imports in a "beggar thy neighbor" policy. The US remained steadfastly isolationist and neutral during the lead-up into World War II (1939-1945). Concerned about Germany taking control of Europe, FDR worked political magic by supplying England with military supplies in the face of much opposition, but the US didn't actually enter the war until Japan attacked Pearl Harbor in late 1941. America's industrial strength was decisive in bringing victory to the allies. All the major industrial powers were left devastated by the war, with just one exception—the United States. (Canada and Australia were also left untouched by the destruction of war, but neither could be counted as a major industrial power.)

After World War II, America adopted a strategy of maintaining its political, military and economic predominance. However, communist Russia seized control of Eastern Europe, developed and deployed nuclear weapons, and built up its military power. Now there were two superpowers—the democratic United States and the totalitarian Soviet Union. To achieve its strategic goal of global predominance, America used two tactics: global engagement and communist containment. Engagement meant maintaining our military strength, developing and strengthening free-market economies, and both creating and leading such international-multilateral organizations as the United Nations, the North Atlantic Treaty Organization, the General Agreement on Tariffs and Trade, the International Monetary Fund, the World Bank, and so forth. Containment meant confronting the Soviet Union in any way possible, from the Berlin Airlift to the Korean War to foreign aid—both military and economic—for friendly countries. We cultivated allies with military protection, economic assistance, and the pursuit of shared political and social objectives. All this was combined with nuclear deterrence, the building up of a large nuclear arsenal and three delivery systems—a long-range bomber force, a ballistic missile submarine fleet, and the dispersal of intercontinental missiles. In essence, our historical practice of post-war reversion to isolationism and disarmament was abandoned.

America followed its strategic policy of maintaining its primary position using the tactics of "containment and engagement" for about four decades under both Democratic and Republican presidents. Lyndon Johnson even went to war in Viet Nam, unsuccessfully and at great cost to this country in terms of lives lost and political dissension. Richard Nixon opened the door to better relations with China, the rising communist power in Asia, as a counterbalance to the Soviet Union. Ronald Reagan built up America's military strength to the point that Russia could not compete and ultimately collapsed economically. This entire period was one of multilateral cooperation and international institutions. A three-pronged approach to foreign policy—containment, cooperation, and institutions backed by American involvement, leadership, economic support and military strength—succeeded in moving the world away from nuclear war and toward democracy and economic prosperity, even in many of the Less Developed Countries.

With the Cold War having been won, the United States was the only superpower with China an emerging power but far behind and Russia a spent power with nuclear weapons. A new bountiful and peaceful world order seemed to be emerging with increasing international cooperation, political democracy and economic globalization. It was not to be. Conflict emerged in Africa, Yugoslavia and the Middle East. Iraq used weapons of mass destruction (poisonous gas) on Iran and its own people and then invaded Kuwait, an important oil producer. President George Bush (the father) built a broad military coalition to drive the Iraqis out of Kuwait. This was a period of political uncertainty as nobody quite knew how to react to the end of the Cold War and the dominant position of the United States, which showed itself to be a reluctant leader, especially under President Bill Clinton, sometimes intervening in smaller wars (Bosnia and Kosovo), sometimes not (Rwanda and Burundi), and sometimes entering and leaving early (Somalia). While world politics was unsettled, however, the world economy prospered with high rates of economic growth in most areas and rapid expansion of world trade.

Then came 9/11. The whole world changed when Al Qaeda brought down the twin towers in New York. President George W. Bush (the son) responded militarily to take out first the Taliban in Afghanistan, which had harbored Al Qaeda bases and leaders, and then oust Saddam Hussein in Iraq, who was thought to be sympathetic to the terrorists and in possession of weapons of mass destruction. There were two major changes in US foreign policy:

- Bush was quite willing for America to go it alone, not waiting for reluctant allies to join forces with this country to achieve key international objectives.

- Bush put the American military on offense rather than defense. America was willing to initiate both preemptive wars (when another country is clearly about to attack) and preventive wars (before another country poses an imminent threat).

The American military had no problem winning the two wars, with widespread international support in Afghanistan and little support in Iraq. However, the United States ended up losing the peace, finding that nation building and bringing democracy to the Middle East both were virtually impossible. To top things off, the American housing sector and overall economy took a hard fall and went into the Great Recession, taking much of the free world with them.

That brings us to the current situation, which can be summed up as sputtering economies, huge private and public debts, Europe in financial crisis, ineffective international cooperation, and President Barack Obama with immense burdens and little chance to find workable and politically acceptable solutions. It seems that virtually everyone, both in America and abroad, has major problems in the short run and much uncertainty about the long run.

OUR FOREIGN POLICY PROBLEMS

America faces a wide range of foreign-policy and national-defense issues. Let's highlight seven of them:

THE MILITARY PROBLEM. This is actually a list of at least four interrelated problems: First, America is fighting a continuing world-wide war against terrorism with no end in sight. Second, America is just now winding down its occupations of Iraq and Afghanistan, but will be maintaining a major commitment in both countries for many years to come. Third, while initial military victory came fairly readily in both countries, we learned not only that our political and military intelligence apparatus is not as good as it needs to be, but also that our military doctrines need improvement. Fourth, we also found that nation building and exporting democracy to foreign nations with no history of democracy is difficult at best and perhaps impossible.

THE ECONOMIC PROBLEM. While America has major domestic economic problems, there are significant international dimensions to our situation. These include:

- a fairly large trade deficit with imports far greater than exports,
- huge foreign holdings of both private and public American debt, with the latter being the larger concern because of the continuing large fiscal deficit and the growing reluctance of foreigners to hold more and more of our obligations, and
- the steady loss of American jobs to the Less Developed Countries (LDCs)—originally blue-collar manufacturing jobs but increasingly white-collar jobs and even high-tech positions.

THE RESENTMENT PROBLEM. America is resented abroad even by our closest allies. In reality, we have many allies but few, if any, friends. Why are we resented? Many people resent America because we have opposed or failed to ratify and participate in such major global treaties as those affecting climate change, nuclear weapons testing and arms trafficking. Many people resent America because we have been willing to go it virtually alone, especially in Iraq and Afghanistan, with little participation of and consultation with our supposed allies. Many people resent America because our culture, thought to be boorish and mundane at best, is spreading rapidly and increasingly dominating the world. Many people resent America because we are the world's biggest polluter, but talk of putting environmental restrictions on the growth of the LDCs. Many people resent America because we have the world's foremost nuclear arsenal but seek nuclear nonproliferation. Many people resent America because we seek free access to markets in the LDCs while protecting our own markets from the agricultural exports of the LDCs so crucial to many poor nations. And the list goes on!

THE DISTRUST PROBLEM. America is feared and not trusted abroad, even by close allies. The US has participated in the overthrow of elected governments that it didn't like (Guatemala and Chile). The US has supported rebel forces seeking the overthrow of other governments it didn't like (Cuba, El Salvador and Nicaragua). The US talks a lot about human rights and the dignity of man while maintaining secret "detention centers" abroad and using questionable interrogation techniques on supposed terrorists. The US talks a lot about freedom while providing the weapons used by some of the world's worst dictatorships to suppress their own people (Saudi Arabia being the leading example). Again, the list goes on!

THE TRANSNATIONAL PROBLEM. Many of our problems and political issues seem to be primarily domestic matters, but in reality have very significant international dimensions. One cannot talk about immigration without mentioning Mexico and Latin America. One cannot talk about our recreational drug problem without mentioning Columbia and Mexico. One cannot talk about energy dependence without mentioning Canada, Mexico and Saudi Arabia. One cannot talk about economic and financial stability without mentioning the euro, China, Japan and Great Britain. In addition, there are major transnational, private organizations, such as Greenpeace and Amnesty International, which have much to say about specific issues. We are not alone!

THE COST OF LEADERSHIP PROBLEM. To become and remain the world's dominant superpower is costly. Economists have long known that there is an inverse relationship between the rate of economic growth and military expenditures. The cost of maintaining a huge military force and fighting two regional wars is not measured just in lives lost, soldiers disabled and large fiscal deficits. It can also be measured in terms of lost opportunities to improve our infrastructure, to spend more on research and development, to undertake and expand worthwhile domestic programs, all of which would make our people better off in the long run. Meanwhile, our allies benefit by not having to do as much while living under the protective umbrella of American power. Fortunately for our politicians, the American voters remain blissfully unaware of the cost they are bearing to maintain American supremacy.

THE GLOBALIZATION PROBLEM. Most people around the world see America as the original and primary source of globalization, which has both major benefits and major costs attached to it. There can be no doubt that it has raised living standards on average around the world, but it also has left many areas behind, unable to compete effectively in a world market. It has increased economic and social inequality both among nations and within nations, as the rich seem to get much richer and the poor fall farther behind. It is a major factor in pollution and resource depletion. It has promoted American-style consumerism and cultural values in many places where they are not wanted, especially by the social and political elites around the world and particularly in the Muslim world.

TERRORISM AND THE UNITED STATES

Terrorism is the systematic use of violent actions to intimidate and create fear in a civilian population and coerce government to change policies. It has been used by a wide range of political (both right-wing and left-wing), nationalistic, religious and revolutionary groups (even governments) to achieve their goals, which usually have been unattainable in more peaceful ways. Terrorism is a pejorative term denoting moral hostility toward whomever is using it. If you oppose the violent actions of a group of dissidents against a government, you call them terrorists; if you support or "understand the reasons for" such violent actions, you call the dissidents "freedom fighters." So Americans have supported the freedom fighters of Libya, Egypt and Syria, but opposed the terrorists of Iraq and Afghanistan.

The United States and other western democracies (England and Spain) have been hard hit by the terrorist actions of Al Qaeda, the radical Sunni Islamic terrorist organization trying to drive western influences out of the Muslim Middle East. The United States, with limited support from other nations, has invaded both Iraq and Afghanistan as part of its fight against Al Qaeda.

We know what Al Qaeda's primary objective is, getting the West out of the Middle East and establishing an Islamic caliphate (pure society). We don't know precisely what its strategy has been and is, but it seems to come down to a series of steps something like this:

1. Provoke the United States into invading Muslim countries;
2. Incite local resistance into using guerrilla warfare against the foreign occupying forces;
3. Expand the military conflict into neighboring countries, forcing the United States to use more of its military forces;
4. Promote having other loosely-affiliated terrorist and guerrilla groups attack America's allies in the hope and expectation that our allies will withdraw support and leave the Middle East;
5. Keep pressure on the United States on a wide range of fronts until Americans tire of the fight and the cost of continuing the conflict becomes prohibitive, so that the United States also eventually withdraws from the fight;

6. Force other sects of Muslims to accede to Al Qaeda, Sunni and Wahhabi (an extremist sect based in Saudi Arabia) leadership; and

7. Install a utopian and radical Caliphate to govern the Muslim world (and ultimately the entire world after Western society and the capitalistic world economy collapses) under strict sharia law passed down from Allah Himself.

This all sounds implausible to us now, but the first five steps are a pretty good description of what happened to Russia in Afghanistan. And we are withdrawing our troops as predicted. And Western society isn't doing that well right now. Gives us something to think about, doesn't it?

The leadership of Al Qaeda has been hard hit, especially by drone attacks. However, the organization is morphing into one that is much harder to deal with. It is hiding out in inaccessible remote areas and failed states. It is allying itself with governments and military forces that share its political philosophy. It has flattened its organization structure, making it harder for us to trace down operating cells. It has trained and collaborated with other terrorist groups who share its hatred of the West. In short, we have chopped off the beast's head, but the beast is alive and still very dangerous.

We have several specific concerns about terrorism:

- There is the danger that terrorists could get control of weapons of mass destruction, especially nuclear explosives from Pakistan, which is unstable and sympathetic to the terrorists.
- Terrorism is spreading to other countries and areas of the world. It isn't just Al Qaeda anymore.
- Home-grown terrorism seems to be on the rise. It is very difficult to detect before terrorist acts take place. Techniques can be learned on the Internet, making traceable visits to training camps unnecessary.
- After a decade with no successful major terrorist attacks at home, Americans are becoming blasé about needed prevention.
- We have had little success in coming to grips with the social and economic conditions that give rise to the distrust and hatred of Western society, especially in the Middle East.

In short, terrorism is still on the front burner.

In 2009, the Department of Homeland Security (DHS) warned that the combination of an economic downturn and election of a black president was cause for increased concerns about right-wing domestic terrorism. Adding to the problem was illegal immigration, increasingly restrictive gun laws, and military veterans returning from the Middle East with psychological problems and strong opinions about Muslims. The warning caused a furor among Republicans that prompted the DHS to disband the unit dealing with domestic terrorism. In a similar vein, the House of Representatives has held several hearings on Muslim terrorism but none on right-wing terrorism. This is in spite of two facts: that if the 9/11 attacks on New York and Washington (a Muslim terrorist act) and the Oklahoma City bombing (a right-wing terrorist act) are excluded, there have been far more right-wing terrorist acts and deaths than Muslim terrorist acts and deaths; and that the number of right-wing, anti-government patriotic groups has risen fairly dramatically. It seems that Americans are much more willing to blame foreigners for domestic terrorism than our own people, thus keeping our heads firmly buried in the sand.

FACTS ABOUT NATIONAL DEFENSE

Let's take a quick look at some readily-available information about the Department of Defense to highlight the magnitude and quality of our military forces.

The United States has a base military budget (excluding the added costs of the wars in Iraq and Afghanistan) of $550 billion a year and has around 1.4 million uniformed troops. This accounts for just under half of the entire world's military spending. The four countries deemed to be potential foes—China, Russia, Iran and North Korea—spend a combined total of $180 billion a year on their military forces, only a third of what we spend, excluding our two wars, which aren't cheap.

The United States has ten naval battle fleets built around large supercarriers—CVN68 through CVN77—with their supporting ships, including nuclear submarines. (CVN68 is scheduled to be decommissioned soon.) The rest of the world has one, and it is under the flag of an ally, Great Britain. China, which is seen as our biggest future competitor and a potential problem, is building its first carrier. Incidentally, America is building two additional, more-advanced supercarriers to join the fleet in 2015 and 2020.

The United States has over 50 attack submarines designed for combat with enemy ships (especially submarines), 14 ballistic missile submarines designed for launching nuclear missiles to serve as a nuclear deterrent, and 4 guided missile submarines designed to attack targets with cruise missiles and to land special forces (Navy Seals) for covert operations.

American troop deployments around the world in late 2011 were well over 50,000 in Germany, just under 40,000 in Japan, just under 30,000 in South Korea, over 10,000 each in Italy and Kuwait, and just under 10,000 in the United Kingdom. Incidentally, the Defense Department has well over 450,000 civilian employees and has local hires abroad of about 200,000.

The Department of Defense acknowledges that it has well over 700 bases abroad but if everything is counted, that number rises to just over a thousand. It operates over 225 golf courses.

American military technology is by far the best in the world. This is the greatest deterrent to major military action by any nation that might think of instigating hostilities against us or our allies. This means that the only wars even vaguely possible are more limited engagements with smaller forces. But even here our technology is inhibiting. One good example of this is the effectiveness of Air Force (and CIA) drones not only in acquiring intelligence but also in finding and taking out terrorist leaders, bases and training camps.

FOREIGN POLICY QUESTIONS

There are numerous foreign policy questions that Americans should be considering. Conservatives and liberals have different responses (using the word "answers" seems inappropriate). Let's ask some pretty important questions, just as American citizens with no special knowledge about foreign affairs and national defense. There are fifteen questions, but we break them into five categories for purposes of organization:

THE FUNDAMENTALS (two questions):

1. What is the purpose of American foreign policy? Is it primarily to protect the American people at home and American interests abroad?

Alternatively, is it to promote freedom and democracy everywhere in the belief that such will be in the long-term best interests of the United States? Throughout the post World War II era, the purposes of American foreign policy were threefold:

- to minimize the risk of military conflict;
- to protect our national security and national interests from the other great and emerging powers (Russia and China); and
- to encourage other nations, especially the LDCs, to develop political, social and economic institutions consistent with American values.

Does this clear-cut set of objectives still apply in the 21st century, now that the US is the only superpower?

2. How should American foreign policy be conducted? Should we go our own way, dealing with each foreign policy issue separately and independently without significant reliance on other nations and maintaining sovereignty and control over the problem? Alternatively, should we work within the context of international organizations, cooperating with other nations to seek worldwide solutions?

OUR BIGGEST FOREIGN POLICY PROBLEMS (two questions):

3. How does the United States protect itself from terrorism? Do we go after the terrorists in their sanctuaries abroad, violating the national sovereignty of other countries? Do we reduce the civil liberties of our own citizens to increase protection within the United States? Do we continue to support dictatorships in the Near East (the primary source of most international terrorism) because they support us and provide us with oil?

4. How does the United States deal with China, increasingly our most important rival? Do we confront China militarily? Do we form alliances to contain China? Do we pressure China about democracy and human rights? Do we restrict trade with China? What do we do if China doesn't want to hold more of our debt?

INTERNATIONAL ECONOMICS (three questions):

5. How does the United States deal with international economic instability? Do we get involved with financial bailouts in the euro zone? Do we coordinate monetary policies with the other economic powers, and do we work through the International Monetary Fund?

6. How does America help the LDCs? Do we free up our domestic agricultural markets, which are well protected, to allow more imports from the LDCs? Do we expand foreign aid, and if so do we help the LDCs with development aid or military assistance?

7. How does America deal with multinational corporations, many of them originating in the United States but essentially independent of any national control? Do we try to regulate them? How can we get them to invest more in this country and hire more American workers? What tax rates do we impose on them?

TRANSNATIONAL PROBLEMS (three questions):

8. What does the United States do about immigration? How do we prevent illegal immigration? What do we do about the millions of illegal immigrants already in the US? How do we encourage immigration of skilled workers and potential entrepreneurs?

9. How does the United States become more energy independent and self sufficient? Do we raise taxes on energy? Do we use regulation or incentives to promote conservation? Where do we locate new refineries? Do we subsidize new technologies to promote alternative energy sources?

10. What does America do about pollution and ecological destruction? How do we reduce our own pollution? How do we encourage other countries to promote abatement? Should America sign international agreements on pollution (the Kyoto protocol)? What, if any, should be our approach to global warming? What do we do to ensure that everyone has sufficient clean water, both here and abroad?

NATIONAL DEFENSE (five questions):

11. How large a military force does America need? What would be the impact of reducing the number of supercarriers by two (20%), the number of attack submarines by five (9%), and the number of ballistic missile submarines by two (14%)? What would be wrong with retiring half the admirals, especially those in Washington? Not to pick on the navy, similar questions could be asked about each of the other services.

12. How many troops does America need to station abroad? Do we really need a thousand bases abroad? What would be the impact of cutting our forces in Germany, the rest of Europe, Japan, South Korea and several other places in half? In some places, altogether?

13. Should the United States work within military alliances (such as NATO) or go it pretty much alone (as we virtually did in Iraq)?

14. Should the United States allow our major allies to freeload on our military strength or should we expect them to pay more for their own protection? Most devote less than half of what we do on defense as a percentage of Gross Domestic Product. Is the current arrangement equitable to us?

15. Should the United States intervene militarily in local disputes between smaller nations or revolutions within nations when we have little directly at stake, even when large numbers of people are being killed or forced to become refugees? Should we intervene only as part of a United Nations peacekeeping force?

ALTERNATIVE APPROACHES

There are two primary schools of thought about American foreign policy—conservative realism and liberal idealism (also called liberal internationalism). Close examination shows that both are closely related to beliefs about domestic policies. Rather than examine them separately, we will look at realists and idealists together, one characteristic at a time.

BASIC PREMISE. Realists are pessimistic. They see human nature as inherently flawed. Both people and nations are selfish, devious and violent. They see a dark world as it is. Idealists are optimistic. They see people and nations as not only able to learn from their mistakes and improve over time, but also cooperative in nature. They see a better and enlightened world.

FUNDAMENTAL APPROACH. Conservative Realists believe that the primary objective of foreign policy should be self-preservation and self-protection. Hence, foreign policy should be defensive and seek the national best interests. It is a zero-sum game in which some countries benefit at the expense of others. Liberal Idealists believe that the primary goal of foreign policy should be to build better relations with other nations. So foreign policy should be cooperative and seeking a better world. It is a positive-sum game in which all nations can benefit.

ACHIEVING PEACE. For realists, we can attain and assure peace in only two ways—either by a balance of power between relatively equal powerful nations, or by being the one and only predominant power. In either case, for realists, the key to having peace is maintaining our military and economic power. For idealists, we can attain and ensure peace through the international cooperation of like-minded nations. Throughout all of history, no democracy has ever gone to war against another democracy. The key to world peace is effective diplomacy and working together through worthwhile international institutions.

NATIONAL DEFENSE. Conservative Realists want to maintain a large and dominating military force with both offensive and defensive capabilities. They want to maintain a large nuclear deterrent. They are willing to sacrifice domestic programs to enlarge our forces and develop evermore effective military technologies. Liberal Idealists prefer a smaller military force, a smaller nuclear deterrent, and a somewhat defensive orientation. They give priority to domestic over military expenditures.

INSTITUTIONS. Realists support military alliances such as NATO which increase American power, have some faith in such international institutions as the IMF where the United States plays a major role, but have little faith in those like the UN where the United States is but one voice among many. Idealists put a lot of faith in international institutions of all types and see them as the foundation for international cooperation.

TREATIES. Conservative Realists have been unwilling to negotiate or ratify major multilateral agreements in some pretty important areas such as ecology, the World Court, and arms limitations. They don't trust other nations and don't want other nations interfering in this country's domestic affairs. They have little faith in multilateral approaches to problem solving. Any international agreement should be in America's best interest. On the other hand, Liberal Idealists see such agreements in a much more favorable light and are far more willing to put the world's best interests ahead of American national interests.

FOREIGN AID. Realists are not very supportive of foreign aid and generally have emphasized military assistance tied to foreign acquisition of American weapons. Idealists have been more willing to help other nations and have put somewhat more emphasis on development and humanitarian aid.

BILL CLINTON V. GEORGE W. BUSH

The last three presidents have been as different from each other as possible with respect to the rest of the world. The result has been wild swings in our approaches to foreign policy. Bill Clinton clearly was a mainstream, middle-of-the-road liberal through his two terms. George W. Bush was a more extreme right-wing conservative during his two terms. Barack Obama would seem to have reverted to being a far left-wing liberal in his term. Perhaps it is too early to give an unbiased evaluation of his foreign policy, so we will add some comments separately. Hence, for now we will confine our discussion to Bill Clinton and George W. Bush.

Bill Clinton was President from 1993 to 2000. His two terms in office were relatively uneventful in terms of international problems. The Soviet Union had collapsed economically and the Cold War was pretty well over. The Middle East continued to be in turmoil, but was no better, no worse than it had been. Clinton's foreign policy can be summed up as:

- promoting freedom and democracy abroad but only with limited commitment by the United States;
- promoting economic development, free trade and international financial stability;
- supporting multinational cooperation primarily through the United Nations and other international institutions;
- supporting international alliances and treaties;
- reducing the national defense budget; and
- involving the United States in foreign crisis situations only when intervention was with international support, morally defensible, and with little risk in terms of American lives and long-term commitments.

In evaluating Clinton's foreign policy you would have to point to his greatest success being in international economics. He was successful in promoting free trade through three major international agreements: the North American Free Trade Agreement (NAFTA) with Canada and Mexico, the General Agreement on Tariffs and Trade (GATT), and the World Trade Organization (WTO). He was also successful in maintaining international financial stability during the currency crises in first Mexico and then Asia. Finally, on the economic front, his administration presided over perhaps one of the longest and strongest periods of sound economic growth and development in modern history, not just in America but around most of the world.

Clinton had some success with peacekeeping interventions in Bosnia and Kosovo, but clear failure in Somalia, and mixed results at best in Haiti. However, his biggest failure perhaps was in doing nothing in Rwanda where about a million people lost their lives in genocidal attacks by their own government. It must be pointed out that the United Nations also failed to act, and Clinton was clearly unwilling to go it alone.

George W. Bush was President from 2001 to 2008. His two terms were far from uneventful, being dominated by American reaction to the September 11, 2001 attacks on New York and Washington, and the subsequent pursuit of Al Qaeda and other terrorist organizations. The focus of foreign policy was on the Middle East. Bush's foreign policy can be summed up as:

- promoting freedom and democracy abroad with military commitment by the United States;
- being willing to go it alone, accepting ad hoc help when offered but not seeking it out;
- going on the offense and being unwilling to adopt just a defensive posture in the War on Terrorism;
- seeking regime change rather than better behavior by foreign governments he openly disliked;
- calling things the way he saw them rather than be diplomatic, using such terms as "evil" and "rogue states";
- downplaying the role of multinational cooperation, the United Nations and other international institutions;
- downplaying the role of international alliances and treaties;
- increasing the national defense budget (over and above the expenses of our two wars); and
- involving the US unilaterally in foreign crisis situations with little regard for international support, the risks to the lives of American soldiers, and the need for long-term commitments, all in the belief that doing so was not just morally defensible but really ethically required of the world's lone superpower.

Evaluating the foreign policy of George W. Bush is extremely difficult. His administration was successful in winning two wars and keeping terrorist acts away from American shores, which is precisely what it sought to do. Yet it is widely thought to have been extremist in nature and a foreign policy failure. Alienating our allies, especially in Europe, will leave scar tissue for many years to come. Going it alone didn't work. Nation building didn't work. Planning for war and ignoring the aftermath didn't work. Staying out of the Kyoto accords and other international agreements has not been helpful. The Bush belief that all that was needed for democracy was getting nations to hold elections has been proven wrong. (Democracy requires guaranteeing personal freedoms and the rule of law as well as developing a needed institutional framework.)

Over time, I believe that we will see a gradual shift away from Conservative Realism toward Liberal Idealism (Internationalism). There are several reasons why this will be the case:

- With the growth of foreign trade, international capital flows, and globalization, the economies of nations are becoming more inter-dependent. What happens in the United States, China and Europe have major repercussions almost everywhere. What happens in other areas and countries have lesser impacts but are still felt over wide areas.
- Globalization and the growing role and power of multinational corporations (MNCs) are forces for international cooperation. These giant firms seek a stable economic environment and easy access to foreign markets. The power of MNCs makes them impervious to the regulation and control of any one nation, even their home country. This means that regulation and control requires countries to work together.
- It is increasingly obvious that many of the world's problems (global warming, resource depletion, poverty, AIDS, terrorism and refugees to name a few) are transnational in nature and cannot be dealt with by any one nation acting alone.
- Democracy is spreading, albeit slowly. People everywhere want solutions to their problems and see cooperation between nations as being the road to improvement.
- The media and especially the internet diffuse information rapidly and universally. Governments everywhere, even totalitarian regimes that try to control the flow of information both into and within their countries, are put under political pressure to pursue the best interests of their people.
- The foreign policy of George W. Bush is widely seen abroad as a failure. There has been a decline of American leadership and a resulting pressure on other nations, especially regionally in Europe and Asia, to work together to solve their common problems.

BARACK OBAMA AND FOREIGN POLICY

It may still be too early to detail and evaluate the foreign policy of President Barack Obama and Secretary of State Hillary Clinton, but we can make some preliminary statements and assessments:

- In 2009, less than five months after taking office, President Obama, speaking in Cairo, Egypt, outlined a new doctrine for American foreign policy. He sought to restore harmony and friendly relations with the Arab and Muslim worlds. He promised "a new beginning" and an era of "mutual respect." His policy of accommodation and concession to the Arab world included an outstretched hand to Iran and Syria, admission for the first time of a major US role in the 1953 coup, a playing down of the Green Revolution, withdrawal without strings from Iraq, a set timetable for leaving Afghanistan, and reduced support for Israel.

- Since the initiation of the Cairo Doctrine, it seems that anti-US sentiment in the Islamic world has increased exponentially. Violence against anything American has risen. The U.S. ambassador to Libya was murdered in Benghazi. The black flag of the Salafist (radical Sunni) jihadist movement linked to al-Qaeda was raised temporarily over our embassies in Tunisia, Egypt, Yemen and Sudan. Clearly, all is not well!

- The Muslim world resists our secular culture on moral grounds. The West continues to be blamed for many centuries of socioeconomic decline and continuing economic exploitation. But a new element has been added. America, the superpower, is in retreat. We are increasingly seen as both weak and unwilling to act. The United States once dominated the Middle East. No more! The four most obvious signs of our changing status are (1) Iran's willingness to defy us by continuing its nuclear weapons program, (2) Pakistan's continuing open support for our opposition in Afghanistan, (3) the ongoing revolutionary strife in Syria, and (4) the growing power of the political Islamists across North Africa, including Egypt.

- Political relations between America and Israel are weakening and becoming strained. Israel wants and probably needs our support and help in dealing with the potential nuclear threat arising in Iran and the continuing conflict with the Palestinians, especially in Gaza. But Obama seems less supportive of Israel than previous presidents.

- President Obama has already indicated that American foreign policy will "pivot" from an emphasis on the Middle East toward more of a focus on Asia and especially our relations with China. On the one hand, this has been greatly facilitated by the changing energy situation in this country as technological change (a process known as fracking) has enabled us to take advantage of our vast underground energy resources. On the other hand, our complicated relationships with China—military rivalry, huge trade deficits, currency "manipulation," and China's immense holdings of American dollars—all point to a need for paying more attention to Asia.

In short, America is the world's only superpower and it has by far the world's strongest and most advanced military forces. Yet, our position in the world—in the Middle East, in Asia, and even in Europe—seems to be fading. Whether this observation is accurate and whether President Obama is culpable in any way remains to be seen. The verdict of history is unknown and before us.

A SIMPLE CONCLUSION

The bottom line on our foreign policy is that it has fluctuated between conservative realism and liberal idealism, sometimes with elements of both at the same time. We have been unable to agree on a single approach. Yet Americans—both politicians and the general population—seem to believe three fundamental things:

1. that the United States has been, is now and always will be a major force for good in this world;
2. that America is and should be the unchallenged world leader; and
3. that virtually all the people of this world want to emulate the American way of life—our democracy, our freedom, our economy, our society and our culture.

For the rest of the world, these three fundamental American beliefs become important questions that might be answered quite differently in various parts of the world: First, is America really a force for good in the world? Second, should America be the world's unchallenged leader? Third and perhaps most important, does the rest of the world want to emulate the American way of life, or would it prefer to pick and choose, emulating some of what we do while avoiding the rest? Given our beliefs and how others respond to those beliefs, can we start to understand why so many people abroad not only see us as being arrogant but are also reluctant to follow our leadership?

7

BIG GOVERNMENT

The appropriate size and role of government is one of the major issues dividing liberals and conservatives. This chapter deals with this controversial matter in some detail, but we must start with some fundamental facts before turning to the more contentious issues. We do this by answering a series of questions:

- How big is government in America?
- What does government do?
- Why has the public sector grown so large?
- What are the limits to the growth of government?

Only then will we look at two issues: the bureaucracy and the size of government.

THE SIZE OF GOVERNMENT

Our government is big. Let's look first at finances. Here are the federal government's 2012 revenues and expenses (in billions):

EXPENDITURES		RECEIPTS	
Social Security	$779	Income Taxes	$1,200
National Defense	$716	Social Security	$841
Income Security	$580	Corporate Taxes	$237
Medicare	$485	Excise Taxes	$79
Net Interest	$225	Other	$147
Education	$139	TOTAL	$2,500
Vet Benefits	$139		
Other	$743	Source: Office of Management and
TOTAL	$3,800	Budget and Time Magazine 9/17/12

This is only part of the picture. There are also tax expenditures in the amount of $1.3 trillion. These are lost tax revenues caused by provisions of the tax laws that allow tax credits, tax deductions, preferential tax rates, and deferrals of tax liabilities. Some of the best-known and most-popular tax expenditures, along with their estimated cost in lost 2012 tax revenues, are employee health-care deductions for business ($184B), the exemption for 401(k) and other savings plans ($138B), the home mortgage interest deduction ($94B), the charitable contribution deduction ($40B), and the deduction for state and local taxes ($37B). Republicans see tax expenditures as a method for increasing business investment and preventing the growth of government by starving it of tax revenue. Democrats see them as a means to channel public money toward social programs—assistance for low-income workers, low-income housing, college tuition, environment-friendly energy, and the like. Reducing or eliminating tax expenditures is no easier than eliminating spending programs. Every tax loophole, no matter how obscure, has large numbers of supporters, and the biggest tax breaks such as those for mortgage interest and employer-paid health insurance, are considered untouchable by politicians.

I use a golf cart for all the golf I play and for running around town occasionally. A couple of years ago, my cart was on its last legs. I went to a local dealer to buy a used but reconditioned gasoline-engine cart. The dealer informed me that the federal government would pay me over $4,000 if I bought a new battery-driven cart. I accepted the dealer's offer for a new "alternative-fuel" golf cart and eventually received a refund check from the Department of the Treasury. I was happy because I got a better product for a lot less money. The government deemed that society was also better off because (1) domestic manufacturing was promoted, and (2) I was using less gasoline with my new "green" vehicle. This is a good example of how the government uses tax expenditures to promote worthwhile and socially-desirable causes.

Now let's look at state and local government revenues and expenditures for fiscal year 2013 (in billions). We round off the figures to the nearest $5 billion for the sake of simplicity:

	STATE	LOCAL
Income Taxes	$330	$ 35
Social Insurance Taxes	$155	$ 5
Ad-valorem Taxes	$495	$495
Fees and Charges	$180	$255
Business and Other Revenues	$395	$265
TOTAL DIRECT REVENUE	$1555	$1060

Source: usgovernmentrevenue.com

	STATE	LOCAL
Pensions	$180	$ 40
Health Care	$465	$135
Education	$295	$645
Welfare	$280	$100
Protection	$ 90	$185
Transportation	$115	$140
General Government	$ 35	$ 55
Interest	$ 45	$ 65
Other	$ 95	$350
TOTAL EXPENDITURES	$1600	$1715

Source: usgovernmentspending.com

Now let's look at government employment. There are about 3 million people working for the federal government, over 5 million for state governments and over 14 million for local governments, giving us a total of about 22.5 million public-sector workers, not including about 2.25 million in our military forces. That means that nearly 7.5% of our population works for government, over 8% if we include our military personnel.

Part of the discussion about the size of government relates to the national debt and other forms of debt. Here are the figures in billions for October, 2012:

Federal Government Debt	$16,135
State Governments Debt	$ 1,095
Local Governments Debt	$ 1,720
Total Personal Debt	$15,830
U.S. TOTAL DEBT	$58,450

Source: U.S. Debt Clock.org

At over $16 trillion, the federal government's debt, what we call the national debt, amounts to over $51,000 per citizen and over $141,000 per taxpayer. Since our Gross Domestic Product is about $15.4 trillion, our national debt is about 104.7% of our GDP. And note that the federal government's debt is greater than the personal debt of all 314.5 million of us.

WHAT DOES GOVERNMENT DO?

Through time, governments have become increasingly important participants in our economy. However, governments interact with the private sector in only seven ways:

- **PURCHASING**. Governments are major buyers of goods and services from the private sector.
- **COLLECTIVE GOODS**. Governments perform functions that are generally not carried out by the private sector: police and fire protection, a court system, a highway system, education, etc.
- **TAXES**. Governments are our tax collectors.
- **TRANSFER PAYMENTS AND SUBSIDIES**. Governments take income from some people and transfer it to other people. They take income from some businesses and subsidize others.

When transfer payments go to low-income people, we call it welfare, and this is what most people think of when they hear the term "transfer payments". But the reality is that a significant portion of transfer payments go to the middle class (e.g., Social Security).

- **COMPETITION**. Governments perform services in competition with the private sector of the economy (e.g., the public utilities).
- **BORROWING**. Government spending is often greater than government revenue, Hence, the public sector regularly borrows money from the private sector (and from abroad).
- **REGULATION**. Governments regulate the private sector of the economy in many ways.

Economists have never agreed on a general method of classification of the functions of government. However, it would seem that there are at least seven economic functions:

1. **PROTECTION**. Governments defend the nation and its people, both collectively and individually, both externally and internally. This involves government in national defense against foreign aggression. It brings the government to the defense of the people against crime, fire, disease, unsafe working conditions and personal contingencies.

2. **LEVEL OF ECONOMIC ACTIVITY**. National governments seek to control the level of economic activity in both the short and long run. In the short run the attempt is to control the business cycle—the level of unemployment and the rate of inflation. In the long run the idea is to increase the rate of economic growth.

3. **SOCIAL GOODS AND SERVICES**. Governments provide social goods and services. Most such products fall into the two areas of social overhead capital (investment in the education and health of people) and infrastructure (investment in transportation, communications and utilities) necessary to private production.

4. **SOCIOECONOMIC ENVIRONMENT**. The public sector establishes the legal and economic environment necessary for a market economy. This environment involves a long list of things we take for granted: a monetary system, a set of standards for weights and measures, corporate laws, contract laws and so forth.

5. **REGULATION**. Governments regulate private decisions, either to prevent the impact of decisions by powerful groups from falling too heavily upon unprotected individuals, or to limit competition because unrestricted competition means low incomes for people.

6. **PROMOTION**. Governments help and promote private enterprise: furnishing credit and subsidies, supplying information and statistics, financing research and development, and using tariffs and quotas to limit foreign competition.

7. **REALLOCATION AND REDISTRIBUTION**. Governments seek to reallocate resources from supposedly less worthy sectors to more worthy sectors of the economy.

This is the most politically sensitive function of government. The problem is that someone in government, sometimes elected representatives and sometimes just appointed bureaucrats, must decide what is good and bad or who is worthy and unworthy.

GROWTH OF GOVERNMENT

The size of government in terms of a greater amount of government spending and more regulation of private economic decisions has steadily increased through time. This expanding economic role of our various governments can be accounted for primarily in eight major factors:

INFLATION. Since World War II, prices in America have risen steadily, at times faster, at times slower.

WARS. A major part of the increase in federal government spending has been to pay the cost of past, present and future wars. If we add together our expenditures on national defense, veterans' affairs, international affairs, space, and interest on the national debt, we would have a fairly accurate picture of the amount of public spending on our various wars.

SOCIAL GOODS AND SERVICES. Rising government expenditures, particularly at the state and local levels, can be accounted for by the fact that the public has demanded more and better social goods and services (highways, schools and parks) as its living standards have improved.

POPULATION GROWTH. An expanding population, especially after the closing of the western frontier, has resulted in a growing need for regulation to prevent one man's attempts to earn a living from interfering with another's. The growing population has also meant a larger number of people to provide social goods and services for.

URBANIZATION. An agricultural society is essentially a self-reliant one, but an urban society needs many services which can only be provided by government.

INDUSTRIALIZATION. The growth of big business has meant that private business decisions generate national impacts. Big business necessitates big government to protect relatively powerless individuals from powerful giant enterprises.

TECHNOLOGICAL CHANGE. The invention and development of new products and processes has necessitated an expanding role for the public sector

SOCIETY'S DECISION. The American people made a major decision during the Great Depression of the 1930s to change the way in which a capitalist economy operates. It was thought that a market-oriented economy has three major shortcomings: inequality, instability and insecurity. The majority of Americans came to support an activist policy to create greater income equality, to bring about greater stability for the economy, and to reduce insecurity in the face of personal contingencies. The result has been growing control of the level of economic activity, the initiation of vast social security programs, and progressive taxation to pay for them.

LIMITS TO GOVERNMENT'S GROWTH

There are limits to the rate at which government can expand and there may even be limits to the ultimate size of government, at least relative to the size of the economy. There are really only two restrictions to the growth and size of government:

THE ECONOMIC LIMITATION. Any economy is restricted by a scarcity of productive resources. There is thus a limit to how much the economy can produce in any given period of time. So there is a real resource cost attached to almost any government action. This real cost of government can be measured by the quantity of private goods and services which could have been produced with the resources used by the public sector. Social goods and services are a substitute for private goods and services in most instances. There are two exceptions to this general rule:

- One exception occurs when the resources used by government would not have been employed by the private sector of the economy. This is one of the main justifications for high government spending in periods of recession; the private sector would not employ the resources involved anyway.
- Another exception can occur with transfer payments. Goods and services are not taken away from the private sector for use in the public sector. Rather, the allocation of goods and services within the private sector is

changed. The public sector is not itself using up resources; instead, it is determining who will ultimately make use of them.

THE POLITICAL LIMITATION. In America, we pay political homage to the ideas of individuality and free enterprise. For this reason, it is politically infeasible to move very quickly away from individuality and free enterprise toward collectivism and public enterprise. Consequently, the growth of government spending and regulation must be a gradual process—evolutionary, not revolutionary. At least in this country, our capitalistic heritage provides a political limitation to the size of government. No politician can advocate the elimination of free enterprise, even though some gradual erosion of the concept may take place over a considerable period of time.

There may be a practical third limit to the size of government, if we believe what we are seeing in Europe. Several countries (Ireland, Portugal, Greece, Spain with Italy and even France in the wings) are facing debt crises as banks and financial markets want to avoid buying their long-term securities. The problem is that their national debt exceeds annual Gross Domestic Product (GDP) and the public sector accounts for over half of GDP (France is over 56%). Each has huge fiscal deficits and little likelihood of any reduction soon as everyone is avoiding market reform and reduced government spending. Is there a lesson here for the United States?

Thus, there are political and economic upper limits to the rate of growth and size of the public sector in our economy. However, there is also a lower limit, provided by the existing role of government. Our various levels of government are heavily involved in economic decisions and the economy. As a practical matter, such government involvement cannot be destroyed. It would be politically and economically impossible to eliminate our social security programs, public education, or the regulation of airline safety. Accordingly, the question which faces us is not the absolute one of how large the role of government should be. Rather, we are faced with the relative question of how much more or less our government could or should be doing.

CONSERVATIVES AND BUREAUCRACY

Conservatives are well known for opposing big government. They believe that the number of workers and the dollar costs are both too high. Why? What are conservatives really saying about government in this country? What is bothering them? Let's take it point by point.

First of all, there are a lot of good people doing good work in difficult and necessary jobs at all levels of government. Conservatives have few, if any, complaints about the jobs being done by teachers, police officers, firemen, highway maintenance workers, prison guards, air traffic controllers, etc. These are the people on the firing line, doing what needs to be done. We need them! No argument!

Second, although conservatives support the vast majority of workers in the public sector, there are some relatively minor abuses associated with these aforementioned workers on the firing line. Some of them receive much higher pay than they would in the private sector. Some get far better pensions and other fringe benefits than they would in the private sector. A few are doing jobs that wouldn't really be needed if they were in the private sector. However, we should note two things:

- These are generally isolated problems and not a big issue in most political jurisdictions.
- These are all diminishing difficulties now that there is so much downward pressure on public sector budgets, especially at the state and local levels.

Living in the Phoenix area with its very hot summers, I am amazed at the private company that collects garbage in our community. Because of the heat, garbage is collected twice a week. Recycling is collected twice a month. That means that my home has collections 128 or 129 times per annum. The men doing the job work harder than anybody I have ever seen doing public service, even running from house to house pushing huge barrels. They are reliable and they take everything. For this year, 2012, we are paying $161 for this high level of service. I defy anyone to find government employees in a metropolitan area providing such good service for this level of cost. And the company is earning a profit. I don't know how, but it is! My point is simply that private enterprise can do many of the jobs done by government, often better and at lower costs. Case closed!

Third, a more significant criticism has to do with the administrative bureaucracies directing the people on the firing line. They are too often too big and too expensive. When our largest public school districts have fewer teachers in the classroom than related service workers and administrators, we don't have our priorities straight. And that is especially true when the teachers are underpaid relative to the administrators directing them, giving good teachers an incentive to leave the classroom in pursuit of more income. Is there any wonder that our students do not score nearly as well on standard tests as students in other countries and that America is falling behind in educating its young people?

Fourth, conservatives recognize that the United States could not be governed without bureaucracies, large and small, at all levels of government. The day-to-day work of the public sector is done by the bureaucracy. Without its hierarchy, chain of command, specialization and division of labor, impersonality, rules, coordination, and written records, the formulation and administration of public policies could not be either effective or efficient. In short, without bureaucracy, governing a nation with about 315 million people would be downright impossible.

Fifth, having made it clear that bureaucracy is necessary for modern government, we conclude there are some very specific problems. The most significant difficulties include:

> Note that the right is most concerned with what happens at the federal level, but these problems can be extrapolated to the lower levels of government. Note also that what is being said about government bureaucracy can equally be applied to private institutions (corporations, charities, nonprofit institutions, etc.), both large and quite small.

TRIADS: Powerful interest groups, Congressional committees and government bureaucracies work together to form triads that control public policy in their specific areas of concern. Outsiders are effectively excluded. The President and White House, given their wider responsibilities and relative lack of specific expertise, usually cannot exert much influence over policy decisions so long as nothing goes wrong and becomes an issue in the media. The experts within the government agencies control both the formation and administration of public policy.

ACCOUNTABILITY: As specialists with many years of experience and lots of contacts, many senior bureaucrats develop the knowledge not only of their subject but also of how the political game is played. Nobody—neither presidents nor oversight committees—can touch them. They are accountable only to themselves. J. Edgar Hoover, Director of the FBI, was the legendary example of this phenomenon.

MEANS BECOME ENDS: All government agencies have goals. They use administrative rules and procedures to achieve their goals. All too often, rather than serving as a means to an end, the rules and procedures become ends in and of themselves.

LACK OF FLEXIBILITY: Bureaucracies develop their own organizational culture and use standard operating procedures, both of which inhibit innovation and change. Once they become established, they become impervious to reform.

GROWTH AND NONREVERSIBILITY: Once formed, a bureaucracy tends to grow. Its mission tends to expand. It competes with other agencies for resources—more personnel and expanded budgets. Senior administrators gain prestige by expanding their agencies. Ultimately, the agency becomes an imbedded part of the Washington landscape with strong allies in both the government and private sector. Its future is assured and it lives forever.

When all is said and done, we all live by a set of laws and rules imposed on us by government. Over time, these laws and rules become more and more stringent. Conservatives have become increasingly concerned that this trend is a threat to our individual freedom. And that perhaps is the essence of the conservative hostility to government.

DEBATE 2012—GOVERNMENT'S SIZE

In 2012, the presidential election campaign between the incumbent Democrat Barack Obama and the Republican challenger Mitt Romney gave rise to a debate on the appropriate size of government. This debate generated more heat than light, but at least it made one think about some of the questions being raised. This section examines some things that should have been said but weren't in order to make readers think about the simple question: What is the appropriate size and role of the public sector in the United States?

The Democrats gained control of the White House, Senate and House of Representatives in the 2008 election. To counteract the Great Recession they inherited, within a month of taking office in early 2009, they enacted an unprecedented spending bill without a single Republican vote. The $787 billion stimulus package amounted to over 5.6% of that year's GDP of just under $14 trillion. There had never been anything like it in absolute size or relative to GDP—not even Roosevelt's New Deal. The stimulus bill may have helped keep us out of a depression, but has been judged to be a political failure because it involved a wide range (some would say a smorgasbord) of programs long on the liberal wish list to change the nature of American society. It spent money on tax incentives, low-carbon pollution abatement, school reform, and health reform as well as creating jobs. The Republicans were highly critical because they believed that:

- many of the programs should have been left to the free market;
- the new technologies that were supposed to materialize were not expected to pan out and didn't;
- much of the money spent was wasted; and
- both school and health reform should have been left to the states.

In short, the Republicans saw the stimulus bill as a boondoggle aimed at increasing the power of the federal government.

Now nearly four years later, our economic situation can be described as a sluggish economy with slow economic growth, high unemployment, a very large and rapidly growing national debt, and a very large fiscal deficit. So what is the problem in Washington? It really comes down to two things:

- With leadership provided by the Democrats, the government has given Americans program after program that provide popular benefits to a very wide range of our people, making promises for the future that it can never deliver on.
- With leadership provided by the Republicans, the government has kept tax rates relatively low and provided taxpayers with a wide range of credits, exemptions and loopholes so that many of our wealthiest people and largest corporations pay little in taxes.

The result has been the development of two very large groups: those who have become dependent on government and don't want to see their benefits reduced, and those who are well off but pay few taxes and resist tax increases. Meanwhile, the middle classes between the two groups—those who receive some of the benefits and pay most of the taxes—are shrinking so that the economic gap between the lower and upper classes is increasing.

The Republican solution to the deficit problem is to cut wasteful non-defense discretionary spending. The problem is that the vast majority of federal spending goes to defense, health care, Social Security, and interest on the national debt. Everything else—what makes up nondefense discretionary spending—amounts to only an eighth of the budget. But the Republicans are unwilling to specify which items within that eighth of the budget they propose to cut for fear of alienating large groups of voters. The Republicans persist in their belief that big government destroys freedom and redistributes income unfairly from deserving, tax-paying citizens to undeserving freeloaders who are little more than wards of the state. Republicans have come to believe that tax cuts are always good, even if they increase the deficit, and government expenditures are always bad, even if they prevent us from falling into a depression. Yet, the Republicans defended President George W. Bush, who started the deficit-debt problem we now face, and are always ready to spend more on national defense and subsidies to big business. What hypocrisy!

The Democratic solution to the deficit problem is to raise taxes on the rich. The problem with this is that doing so will not reduce the deficit significantly unless the tax cuts are large enough to affect incentives to work and invest significantly. The Democrats never saw a government domestic spending program or tax increase for the middle and upper classes that they didn't like. They are against either reduction or reform of the major programs that are the source of our deficit problem—Social Security, Medicare and Medicaid. They are opposed to modernizing government to increase its productivity and doing anything to annoy the public-sector unions and public employees, who are on average better paid and have more fringe benefits and security than private-sector workers.

Then there is the problem of government regulation of private business. The number of regulators and regulations has been increasing rapidly under the Obama administration, especially in Homeland Security and Environmental Protection. And the full impact of the legislation that will increase regulation most of all has yet to hit—Obamacare and the Dodd-Frank financial reform. The Democrats say that they support free enterprise and free markets, but the truth is that they don't trust business people and anybody they cannot control. Again, what hypocrisy!

Finally, there is difficulty with our senior citizens. The problem is that they are living longer, retiring earlier, demanding higher Social Security benefits and better health insurance, and opposing almost anything else, especially higher taxes And they vote in large numbers. Neither political party is willing to say no to them. There is no solution to our deficit and debt problems that will not infuriate large numbers of seniors. That fact alone prevents Washington from doing anything meaningful to resolve our fiscal dilemma.

The problem is NOT that we don't know what needs to be done, but that our politicians are unwilling to act in the best long-term interests of the country. Washington is gridlocked. The bipartisan Bowles-Simpson commission produced a reasonable recipe for reform: short-term stimulus to bolster the economy, long-term entitlement reform to lower the deficit, and simplification of our tax code. Both parties rejected it. Neither offered reasonable alternatives, both sticking to their ideological talking points to appease their members. Sooner or later, America will have to do something. We cannot continue to borrow from abroad to pay for our deficit. The Republicans will have to accept higher taxes, tax reform and reduced spending on national defense; the Democrats will have to accept entitlement reform and reduced spending on domestic programs. And seniors will have to accept that the rationing of healthcare and postponing of pensions are both inevitable.

This came off the internet in late 2012. I have no idea who wrote it, but it is good at putting our fiscal problems in perspective.
* U.S. Tax revenue: $2,170,000,000,000
* Federal budget: $3,820,000,000,000
* New debt: $1,650,000,000,000
* National debt: $16,271,000,000,000
* Recent budget cuts: $38,500,000,000
Let's now remove 8 zeros and pretend it's a household budget:
* Annual family income $21,700
* Money the family spent: $38,200
* New debt on the credit card: $16,500
* Balance owing on the credit card: $162,710
* Total budget cuts so far: $385
Maybe now we can all see the problem.
Nobody will like what is coming. America has been living beyond its means. We have taxed ourselves as a miserly nation; we have spent money as a profligate nation. That era is over. Whether or not we can and will accept this reality is unknown. Stay tuned! America is at risk!

8

HISTORY, PROBLEMS, OBJECTIVES

This chapter is broken into four sections. The first provides a very brief historical background on the presidency for the past eighty years. The second looks at how through time liberalism has taken over this country. The third section briefly discusses six long-term problems presently facing America. The fourth looks at society's major economic objectives.

THE PRESIDENCY—A HISTORY

We are going to examine the sweep of modern American political history in order to prove two points:
- that conservatives and liberals, Republicans and Democrats are about evenly balanced, neither dominating the other; and
- that the presidency often changes party hands because of the failures and excesses of the incumbent party.

We will do this by election years:

1932-1952. These were the Democratic years of Franklin Delano Roosevelt and Harry Truman, brought to power by the Great Depression and the inability of the Herbert Hoover administration to deal with it. This followed a long period of Republican control. Oddly, Roosevelt was elected on a fairly conservative platform, but soon converted his policies toward liberal interventionism.

1952-1960. This was the Republican time of Dwight David (Ike) Eisenhower, a war hero and moderate who readily defeated a tired Democratic Party, in part with the promise of ending the war in Korea.

1960-1968. These were the Democratic years of John Fitzgerald Kennedy and Lyndon Baines Johnson. Kennedy was a moderate Democrat who was elected because Eisenhower failed to deal successfully with three recessions in eight years. Johnson, who took over after Kennedy's assassination, was originally thought to be reasonably conservative for a Democrat, but then came to be seen as one of our most liberal presidents because of his Great Society. In 1964, Johnson easily defeated Barry Goldwater, the right-wing conservative candidate, who rejuvenated conservatives and opened the door for future conservative candidates.

1968-1976. Now it was the turn of the Republicans again with Richard Nixon readily winning the presidency because Lyndon Johnson lost his popularity over the Vietnam War. Gerald Ford became president when Nixon resigned because of the Watergate scandal. Both Nixon and Ford were seen as middle-of-the-road, moderate or even liberal Republicans, with Nixon being seen as slightly more conservative.

1976-1980. Because of Republican scandals, Americans made Jimmy Carter, a moderate Democrat, president.

1980-1988. In the face of foreign policy failures in the Middle East and stagflation—the combination of recession and inflation—under Jimmy Carter, Ronald Reagan became the first truly conservative modern Republican president.

1988-1992. Given Reagan's popularity because of a strong economy and the collapse of Russian communism, Vice President George Bush, a moderate Republican, was elected as his successor.

1992-2000. Because his Republican predecessor failed to take significant action against recession at the end of his term, a moderate Democrat, Bill Clinton became president. During his eight years, he brought the Democratic Party further to the right than any of his predecessors. He cut taxes, balanced the federal budget, moved America toward free trade, and did not undertake any new social programs, although he did seek medical reform early on.

2000-2008. In the closest election in American history, George W. Bush, running as a compassionate conservative, won the presidency, in part because of the sex scandals of Bill Clinton. Bush turned out to be anything but a conservative, running huge fiscal deficits, initiating the first new entitlement program in over a quarter of a century, increasing spending on domestic welfare and foreign aid, and getting America involved in two wars at the same time.

2008-Present. Running against the foreign entanglements, huge deficits, and economic problems of George W. Bush, Barack Obama easily won the presidency for the Democrats. He was the most extreme liberal to have become president in the modern era. His passage of medical care legislation, generally known as Obamacare, without a single Republican vote, coupled with continuing economic problems and large fiscal deficits, gave Republicans hope for the 2012 elections, but the President was reelected fairly easily.

The Democrats held the presidency in twelve of the last twenty-one terms and dominated both the early years and recent times. The Republicans held the presidency for the other nine terms and dominated the middle years.

Looking at the decisive factors when the presidency changed parties, we can say that economic problems were a major factor in the elections of Roosevelt (1932), Kennedy (1960), Reagan (1980), Clinton (1992) and Obama (2008). Scandals were an important factor for Carter (1976) and Bush (2000). War and foreign policy were significant for the elections of Eisenhower (1952), Nixon (1968), Carter (1976), Reagan (1980) and Obama (2008).

With this as background, let us look at how the Democratic Party has changed in four stages over the years:

THE NEW DEAL: 1932-1952. A coalition of the white working class, unions and the south was the foundation of the Democratic Party, which stood for new government programs and spending to help lower-income groups, support for unions, regulation of business, and acceptance of traditional morality. This became known as the era of the Old Democrats.

THE GREAT SOCIETY: 1960-1968. People in the white working class and south became alienated and deserted the Democrats in droves because of the cultural convulsion that accompanied the movement of their party toward ethnic minorities and civil rights, student and anti-war activists, environmentalists, and feminists. This was a transition era for the Democratic Party, moving it to the political left. The white working class, which had been the very foundation of the Party, was hostile to the new social movements and left the Party in large numbers. Feminism was identified with hostility to the family; the antiwar movement with appeasement; and environmentalists with opposition to economic growth. The Old Democrats no longer fitted in.

CLINTON AND THE DEMOCRATIC LEADERSHIP COUNCIL: 1992-2000. The DLC and Bill Clinton's administration supported fiscal conservatism (a balanced budget), welfare reform, anti-crime programs (longer mandatory sentences, capital punishment and more police presence), and support for traditional families. This was an attempt to form a new coalition by regaining the support of Old Democrats while retaining that of the various movement activists from the Great Society era. This became known as the era of the New Democrats.

OBAMA AND THE EXTREME LEFT: 2008-PRESENT. Barack Obama is the most extreme left-wing and radically liberal president America has ever had. Having inherited a major domestic economic crisis and two wars in the Middle East, his administration operated with a humongous fiscal deficit, took control of failing large manufacturing firms, tremendously increased the regulation of business and especially larger financial firms, enacted major changes in how America acquires medical care, and started to reduce America's dominant leadership role in the international community.

Over time, we could judge that the Democratic Party has gone through four stages—from traditional liberalism to extreme liberalism to moderate liberalism and finally to radical liberalism.

The Republican Party has also changed significantly over the years, primarily in terms of its ideology. The Eisenhower administration (1952-1960) was pro-business and moderate, not seeking significant changes in the welfare state created by the New Deal. With the nomination of Barry Goldwater in 1964, the party turned to extreme conservatism. Four years later the Republicans turned to Richard Nixon, a moderate but pragmatic conservative. The Reagan-Bush administration was ideologically very close to being a pure conservative one, but in practice was flexible and pragmatic. George W. Bush described himself as being a compassionate conservative, but in reality turned out to be a neoconservative who not only supported a robust military and foreign policy, but also abandoned traditional conservative domestic policy ideals, running large fiscal deficits and initiating the first new domestic entitlement program in a quarter of a century. After Bush, the Republican Party gradually moved in a more extreme conservative, almost reactionary, direction, not being willing to compromise on its principles. Oddly enough, while becoming more rigidly conservative and after losing the presidency with a moderate in 2008, the Republicans stayed with a moderate candidate and losing strategy in 2012.

THE LIBERAL TAKEOVER OF THE U.S.A.

All conservatives believe that this country's standards of morality and behavior have worsened in modern times. The values of our forefathers, which were the very foundation of American culture and had stood the test of time for nearly two centuries, were virtually destroyed in the 1960s. Liberalism took over the United States, its values, its culture, its politics and its government. This section will examine the liberal takeover of this country and in doing so will seek to answer three questions:

- What enabled liberalism to successfully take control of public policy in America?
- How did liberalism take control of American public policy?
- What was the impact of liberalism's takeover in the US?

Liberalism's attaining of a dominant political position in this country required Americans to develop a confident belief that the government, and especially the federal government, was able to do good for the vast majority of people. They had to come to the belief that big government was good government. Through much of our history, Americans not only distrusted government but also supported a small and limited public sector. That all changed, beginning in the 1930s. There were several reasons why Americans came to believe in big government:

- Most Americans believed that government programs under Franklyn Roosevelt's New Deal were responsible for bringing America out of the Great Depression.
- Big government, in cooperation with big business, was clearly responsible for winning World War II.
- Big government was believed to be responsible for unprecedented prosperity after World War II.
- Nearly two decades of Cold War success conditioned most Americans to rely on and trust the central government to solve their most serious problems.

As a direct result of these four major successes, public confidence in government, especially the federal government, came into being.

We can see the process of liberalism and big government taking over the United States as a series of six overlapping and interrelated steps. The first was the emergence of a liberal elite. It came to dominate the universities (especially in the social sciences and humanities), the media, entertainment (especially in Hollywood and New York), the publishing industry, the legal profession (especially our most prestigious law schools and many of our higher-court judges), some of the liberal Protestant churches, and much of the federal government bureaucracy. This elite was confident in its belief that it knew what was best for American society. It had the platform and ability to dominate the discussion of our major economic, social and political issues.

The second step in the process of liberalization took place under President John Kennedy. Eisenhower, his predecessor, had passively accepted slow economic growth and three minor recessions in his eight years. Kennedy, elected on a platform of getting this country moving again, assumed responsibility for using fiscal policy to prevent unemployment and increase the rate of economic growth. Adopting Keynesian economic theory, Kennedy accepted responsibility for managing the aggregate economy. When prosperity ensued, macroeconomic policy became a stable part of the public sector's responsibility.

The third step in the process involved Supreme Court rulings on the separation of church and state. The First Amendment to the Constitution forbids Congress to make any law "respecting an establishment of religion" and "impeding the free exercise of religion." (It also protects freedom of speech, freedom of the press, the right to peaceably assemble, and the right to petition the government for redress of grievances.) It is clear that the original purpose of the First Amendment was to prevent any state (or the federal government) from establishing a state religion—a common practice in Europe where they have such things as the Church of England. Nevertheless, the Supreme Court created a total wall of separation between church and state to effectively ban public prayer and religious readings in school. Over time, this has morphed into extreme bans on everything from displays of the Ten Commandments and religious Christmas decorations to not allowing any publicly-owned facilities to be used for religious purposes, broadly defined.

The fourth step was another set of Supreme Court rulings, this time on the very nature of the Constitution of the United States of America. When its own legal precedents prevented it from eliminating segregation, the Supreme Court ruled that if the Constitution couldn't be used to provide absolutely necessary relief, the Constitution itself would have to accede to society's current needs. We went from literal interpretation of the Constitution (strict construction) to the Constitution being seen as a living document subject to the changing needs of modern society. This interpretation opened Pandora's Box to liberal judges becoming social reformers. The courts could now achieve social, economic and political change that would not have been possible through legislative or administrative action.

The fifth step in the liberalization process involved three specific changes in the Supreme Court's interpretation of the Constitution that transferred power from the states to the federal government:

- The "general welfare" clause was used to allow Congress to allocate funds for any purpose it wanted with no regard for Constitutional limits on Congress.
- The "interstate commerce" clause was broadened to allow federal regulation of anything that affects interstate economic activity, even if nothing crosses state lines.
- The "due process" and "equal protection" clauses were expanded upon to allow the federal government to regulate both education and criminal law.

As a result of these Supreme Court rulings and others like them, the federal government became all powerful and had the final say on most public policies. State and local governments became minor players in the political game.

> Given steps three through five of the liberalization process, is it any wonder that many conservatives, who would prefer a much smaller federal government with limited powers, so bitterly dislike the Supreme Court!

The sixth and last step involved legislation passed under Lyndon Johnson's Great Society, which marked the high point of American liberalism. The key legislation included the following:

- The Civil Rights and Voting Rights Acts moved race relations from the state to the federal venue.
- Medicare and Medicaid brought the federal government into the health-care business.
- The War on Poverty had the government redistributing income and wealth from the upper to the lower classes.
- The Elementary and Secondary Education Act, the Higher Education Act, and Head Start gave Washington a major say in education, previously reserved to state and local governments.

The liberal takeover of the United States was now complete.

The increasing domination of big government and liberalism had a major impact on moral values and culture in America. Senator Jim DeMint (Rep-SC) and Dr. David Woodard (Clemson University) described the effects as follows:

(There are) two very different worldviews about moral authority—the basis by which people determine whether something is good or bad, right or wrong, acceptable or unacceptable:

- orthodox traditionalism—a commitment to consistent, unchangeable measures of value, purpose, goodness and identity;
- progressive modernism—defined by the spirit of the age, a spirit of rationalism and subjectivism. [1]

This country has moved steadily from orthodox traditionalism to progressive modernism. It has rejected long-accepted moral absolutes and social institutions in favor of the new moral relativism and emphasis on the individual. Gone are our time-tested beliefs in sexual fidelity, strong family ties, civic organizations, churches, honesty, service to mankind, responsibility, and a strong work ethic. These have been replaced by the acceptance of premarital sex, abortion, same-sex marriage, no-fault divorce, single-parent families, legalized drugs, pornography, and welfare handouts.

Conservatives believe in moral absolutes, religious values, and strong social institutions. They feel that these things are important in restraining mankind's destructive tendencies and improving human behavior. They consider these things to have been crucial to America's strength and supremacy, confirmed by several centuries of history. They fear that the rise of moral relativism, the decline of religious belief, and the withering of our social institutions will weaken and perhaps ultimately destroy our society and our nation.

LONG-RUN PROBLEMS

Since the start of the 21ˢᵗ century, American voters have been faced with six very significant and increasingly obvious problems that aren't going away and which neither political party seems to have reasonable answers for:

1. **The Economic Performance Problem**: the growing instability and slowing of the American and international economies;

2. **The Inequality-Poverty Problem**: the growing inequality in both income and wealth between the upper and lower classes, combined with the increasing poverty of the lower classes and the gradual decline of the middle classes;

3. **The Deficit-Debt Problem**: the growth of fiscal deficits and the national debt;

4. **The Education Problem**: the steady deterioration of education in America and the ability of our young people to compete for high-income jobs;

5. **The Family-Morality Problem**: the steady deterioration of the American family and morality in our American culture; and

6. **The Middle East Problem**: the continuation of American participation in endless wars and involvement in the instability of the Middle East.

Neither Republican conservatives nor Democratic liberals seem to have solutions for any of these problems. Heck, they don't have any practical suggestions! All they do is blame each other and refuse to work together to get anything meaningful accomplished. Let's look at the six problems in more detail:

ECONOMIC PERFORMANCE

When faced with the question of how to promote prosperity in the short run and increase the rate of economic growth in the long run, Conservatives and Republicans have always given the same answer: cut taxes and reduce regulation. This response is clearly inadequate in the face of three facts: that our personal tax rates are relatively low; that we have large fiscal deficits; and that we have been through a period of significant deregulation. We now have to think more in terms of:

- finding ways to increase government revenues, probably through higher taxes on households, in order to reduce the fiscal deficit, which cannot be sustained in the long run; and
- increasing business investment incentives on the supply side more than increasing household consumption on the demand side.

In any case, the time for broad middle-class tax cuts, no matter how politically popular, are over. We need a new conservative and Republican economic agenda. As for the liberal and Democratic economic agenda, there is virtually none. All that has been proposed is to spend more on transfer payments to the poor and raise taxes on the rich.

INEQUALITY AND POVERTY

The long period of economic prosperity that began in Ronald Reagan's presidency and continued well into the George W. Bush presidency with little interruption was very good for the upper classes and okay for the middle classes, but did little for the lower classes. The result was increasing inequality in the distribution of income and wealth combined with a persistent (perhaps accelerating) poverty problem. What little debate there has been about the problem has not been very helpful.

We know a lot about the causes of the problem. Columnist Michael Gerson[2] has said that failing families are a combination of interrelated problems; that globalization and new technology put downward pressure on wages and lead to stagnant labor markets; that permissive cultural norms encourage family breakdown and self-destructive behavior; and that the modern welfare state is not focused on empowering the poor, but instead, has increased the percentage of government transfer payments going to middle- and upper-income seniors. The liberal mantra is that the rich should pay higher taxes to provide more money for the poor. Conservatives believe that this would not work and suggest that more jobs for lower-income people is the ticket, without offering any suggestion as to how such jobs would be created beyond their usual incantation of lower taxes and less regulation.

Gerson continued by stating that focusing on concrete solutions to specific problems often is effective. He gave four examples of things that worked and positively affected millions of low-income families. Welfare reform reduced social-worker caseloads while increasing employment and income for low-income families. Community policing and zero-tolerance policies reduced crime. The Supplemental Nutrition Assistance Program, which reformed the food-stamps program, has reduced hunger. The earned-income tax credit has encouraged work and reduced poverty. These smaller steps, all with bipartisan support, were successful. Yet, our two political parties now bicker and do virtually nothing, even though the American public has expressed its concern and even outrage.

DEFICITS AND THE DEBT

President Obama commissioned the Simpson-Bowles Deficit Reduction Committee not long after taking office. The Committee issued a detailed report on how the fiscal deficit could be eliminated over time, primarily by fixing our major middle class transfer payment programs (Social Security and Medicare) and closing a wide range of tax deductions and loopholes that benefit the middle and upper classes. The President completely ignored the report, as did Congressional Democrats and Republicans. Nobody in Washington is at all serious about tackling the related problems of the large fiscal deficit and the growing national debt.

Columnist Robert J. Samuelson[3] showed how America is shifting away from "give-away to take-away politics." Since World War II, Congress has been able to provide people with a wide range of benefits, many in the form of transfer payments for the middle class, without raising taxes. These give-aways were made possible by reduced defense spending and rapid economic growth. This era is over because of slower economic growth, an aging population, and rising health costs. Congress is now facing the need for reduced benefits and higher taxes—politically unpopular take-aways. Economic conditions have changed, but political circumstances haven't. Democrats still want more spending; Republicans more tax cuts. Neither is willing to seek any compromise. The result is impasse. And America suffers.

Two things are inevitable: reduced benefits in our major transfer programs and higher taxes. When these will happen is impossible to guess, but eventually they will take place. Since income, wealth and corporate taxes all have negative incentive effects on work, saving and investment, it seems likely that Congress will turn to a different form of taxation, the value added tax (VAT), which is essentially an excise tax on production. It is used in most other advanced economies and thus we know what it will do. It is effective in raising revenue but has smaller impacts on incentives to work, save and invest. Republicans hate the VAT because it is so effective in raising tax revenue. Democrats hate the VAT because it is regressive, having larger impacts on lower-income groups than on higher-income groups.

EDUCATION

Not only is the American system of public education failing us, but it is also gradually but steadily getting worse. There are major performance issues as American students are falling farther behind students abroad, especially in mathematics, science, and writing skills, making our future labor force less able to compete in an increasingly worldwide labor market. Most universities, even the elite ones, are forced to offer large numbers of remedial classes to make up for the failures of our high schools. Too many students are lazy and take the easy way out by enrolling in easy, irrelevant courses, especially in universities that offer a smorgasbord of subjects to maintain enrollments. Modern students are not being taught enough about religion, morality, and our history to make them good citizens; in fact, cheating and plagiarism are rampant. Too many classrooms provide a lousy learning environment because they are too often violent and distracting since teachers are not allowed to control and discipline their charges, and teachers are forced to spend too much time on the poorest students, many immigrants with language problems. Bad teachers are protected by tenure, seniority and union rules while good teachers tend to quit early because of long hours, low pay, frustration, stress and lack of support from either supervisors or parents.

We all know the problems and the causes. Parents are not involved enough in the education of their children; they are not pushing homework; they are not requiring better subject choices and better grades; and they are allowing their children to watch too much TV. Bureaucracy rules the roost in education, especially in our largest school districts, and puts far too much emphasis on educational processes rather than educational results. The federal government has become heavily involved and provides enough financing to ensure that it can maintain control everywhere; the result is too much bureaucracy, too much regulation, too rigid personnel rules, too much teacher union lobbying, too much of a civil-service mentality, too much social engineering, too much politics, and too little local discretion and experimentation. There is no consensus on either what students should be learning or how policies should be tailored to specific situations.

After looking at the problems and their causes, we can enumerate a few of the major suggested solutions to our education problems. They include a more rigorous curriculum, more frequent student assessment, continuing teacher development, an ability to eliminate bad teachers, more parental involvement, competition from private and charter schools, more local control, and a reduced size of the educational bureaucracy.

And we have just scratched the surface of the education problem in the United States.

THE FAMILY AND MORALITY

Family structure in America is changing. The nuclear family—father, mother and children, sometimes with grandparents living in the home—is no longer the norm. Singles, single parents, cohabitation, and gay couples (some with children) have become commonplace. The causes are well known: the rise of individualism, materialism and secularism; women's and sexual liberation; and readily-available divorce and abortion. The adverse results are also pretty obvious: more family breakups, more poverty, more teen pregnancies, more illegitimate births, more obscenity, more school dropouts, more drugs, and more crime. The psychological problems are also there. The single parent has nobody there for mutual support to share her (sometimes him but usually her) problems with, and often has money problems and difficulties balancing work and family.

Liberals and conservatives have widely divergent views about all this. Liberals accept sexual liberation and nontraditional families, and want to adjust public policies to provide financial aid for low-income nontraditional families, to allow adoption by single parents and gay couples, to require sex education in our elementary schools, to support abortion, and to provide contraception in our high schools. Conservatives oppose all of the above and support traditional marriage, sexual abstinence outside of marriage, and bans on abortion. This is the crux of what has come to be called the "culture wars" or "social issues" in America.

At the start of the 2012-2013 TV season, USA Weekend for September 14-16 ran a cover on "The New TV Family" and an accompanying article entitled "The Postmodern Family." It talked about the new family shows for the upcoming season, highlighting a single woman raising a child, a brother-sister household, families with divorced and stay-at-home fathers, adult children moving back in with their senior parents, a gay couple with an adopted child, and a gay male couple that hires a surrogate to bear their baby. This is what is thought to be "The New Normal," which is the title of one of the shows. The traditional family of a married couple with children is out; different types of families, far from traditional, are in. Of course, most liberals think all this is quite acceptable, but many conservatives (perhaps most and especially those on the religious right) are incensed, believing that this is just one more indication of America's moral decline.

THE MIDDLE EAST

The United States has a continuing problem with the Middle East. In reality, the concern is with a broader area stretching from Libya in North Africa to Pakistan in Asia. There are at least eight major areas of concern:
- War: We have fought three wars there, twice with Iraq and once with Afghanistan. The costs of all three have been huge in terms of lives lost (both ours and theirs), resources and our international reputation. The gains have seemingly been minimal.

- Military Commitment: We maintain an ongoing and permanent commitment to the military safety of Israel, Kuwait and Saudi Arabia. We also have implicit commitments to other countries in the region.
- The Coming of Democracy: The Arab world is starting to become more democratic, with Libya and Egypt being in the forefront. The US supports democracy in the Middle East, but we may well find that the resulting governments are not that supportive of capitalism and freedom as well as being somewhat unfriendly toward us. We support democracy but may not like its results.
- Dependence on Persian Gulf Oil: The United States doesn't get that much of its oil directly from the Persian Gulf, but oil is a world market and we are affected by what happens there since the entire world depends on oil from the Middle East.
- International Capital Flows: All that oil flowing out of the Middle East means that there are huge capital flows into such countries as Saudi Arabia and Kuwait. What the governments of these countries do with all that money affects the world economy and international financial system, both of which are relatively fragile.
- Terrorism: The Middle East is the source of Muslim terrorism, its leadership, its troops, its training facilities, its financing and its hideouts. Much of its inspiration comes from the largest oil provider, Saudi Arabia, and its Wahhabi religious sect.
- Failed States: There are several failed states in the Middle East with Yemen being the most obvious example. The problem is that there are several other nations, some large and important, that can be described as being close to failed states.
- Nuclear Weapons Development: We know that Israel and Pakistan have nuclear weapons and that Iran is building up a nuclear potential. One concern is that the governments and military leaders of these nations might be quite willing to use nuclear weapons. Even more of a concern is the possibility of terrorist groups getting control of weapons of mass destruction; we know they would be willing to use such weapons, no matter what the cost.

Because of the Middle East, America and the West seems destined to live out the Chinese curse: "May you live in interesting times."

Many Americans believe that we have a China problem that is not that dissimilar from our Middle East problem. There is no doubt that China gives us economic, political and military difficulties; it is a very tough adversary. However, there is a difference for two reasons. First, China has many of the same problems we do: an aging population, international trade and financial imbalances, competition from other countries with lower labor costs, inadequate energy resources, pollution, etc. Second, we can treat China as a rational nation acting in its own self-interest. We really cannot do that in the Middle East as far too often the citizens and governments there act irrationally, at least from our perspective. We have trouble understanding their actions and ways of thinking. Heck, we even have trouble dealing with the Israelis, and they are our closest allies in the Middle East.

ECONOMIC OBJECTIVES

Society's economic goals can be classified into five broad categories: economic stability, economic growth, economic efficiency, economic security, and economic freedom. Let's discuss each in turn.

ECONOMIC STABILITY

The economic stability objective has two dimensions—full employment and price stability.

Full employment means the maximum utilization of all our input resources—labor (including entrepreneurship), capital, and natural resources. While it applies to all inputs, it is usually thought of in terms of labor. For workers and business leaders not to be fully employed currently means that their potential output is lost forever. This is not necessarily true of the other resources, as natural resources and capital equipment can be used in the future if left unused in the present, although capital equipment can become obsolete and thus unusable. For people, full employment cannot be equated with zero unemployment. Since an economy is dynamic and continually changing, some resources are always between uses. When there is full employment, some people are between positions in the process of resource reallocation, necessary in an economy that is continually changing. However, the number of people unemployed but seeking work is equal to the number of unfilled job openings. It takes time to match up the unemployed with the job openings. The more dynamic the economy, the higher the acceptable or full employment level of unemployment will be. Since the United States is the world's most dynamic economy, it has the highest level of unused resources consistent with full employment. Hence, we are thought to be at full employment in the United States when between 4% and 6% of our workers and between 12% and 15% of our capital resources are idle.

Originally our price stability objective meant the avoidance of both inflation and deflation. Over time, this has reverted to concern primarily about inflation as deflation was thought by economists and our political leaders to not be feasible in a modern society. This, however, has changed as Japan has experienced a long period of deflation, while both Europe and America have become increasingly concerned that their economies could slowly deflate. Inflation is a general increase in the level of prices, and can also be thought of as a general reduction in the value of money. (Of course, deflation is a general reduction in the level of prices and a general increase in the value of money.) Note that price stability does not mean that all prices remain constant, but that some prices are rising and some prices are falling such that on average prices remain fairly steady. This means that people with a steady money income are neither better off nor worse off when there is price stability. Their real income measured in terms of the goods and services they can buy remains approximately constant.

ECONOMIC GROWTH

Economic growth is an increase in the economic welfare of the average individual in society. Since how well off people are is not improved by rising prices, growth must be measured in terms of the real output of goods and services. Since rising real output can also be offset by increases in population, economic growth is measured in real output per capita. Besides allowing for rising prices and rising populations, there are other problems with measuring economic growth:

1. Not all we produce can be used for current consumption without jeopardizing future consumption. Some of what we produce today must be used to replace the capital equipment used up in current production.

2. Likewise, some of what we produce today should be used to maintain the quality of our physical and social environments. Our economic welfare is determined not only by the quantity of goods and services we consume, but also by the nature of society within which we live. In short, we must consider the quality of life.

3. Not all increases in production and consumption make us better off. Some are used to offset the negatives in society. Thus, national defense, police protection and government regulation might be thought of as not adding much to making us better off. They just prevent us from becoming worse off.

4. The distribution of income and wealth is highly controversial when we think of economic growth. If the vast majority of any increase in a nation's production and income goes to a small upper-income elite, which already holds most of the wealth, is society really experiencing economic growth?

ECONOMIC EFFICIENCY

Economic efficiency is known to economists as an efficient allocation of resources. It means providing consumers with the goods and services they want at the lowest possible real resource costs and at the lowest sustainable prices. Giving people what they want has two important implications:

1. Economists attach no moral judgments to specific products. All goods and services are considered equal providing that one person's acquisition and consumption of them does not adversely affect the well-being of another. In short, people should be free to make their own choices so long as they do not impose significant costs on others.

When I was teaching, I used to get a good discussion going by asking students whether buying marijuana was that different from buying textbooks. After all, buying marijuana can meet the two criteria of free choice and not affecting others. There is also the related question of the difference between alcohol (which is legal) and marijuana (which is illegal). It has always been amazing to me how many people in our society want to tell others how to live their lives and what they should do with their money.

2. Providing consumers with what they want requires that the production be flexible and responsive to changes in consumer tastes and preferences. This requires that input resources be readily mobile between employments. In short, supply must respond to changes in demand.

Cost minimization has three significant implications:

1. The state of technology must improve over time. Society should have strong producer incentives to promote technological change, which has three dimensions: invention (the expansion of knowledge), innovation (the application of knowledge), and diffusion (the dissemination of knowledge).

2. All factors of production must be used in their best possible applications. For this reason discriminatory practices that keep certain groups of people out of positions for which they are qualified tend to cause economic inefficiency as well as social injustice. Likewise, using taxes and subsidies to move resources out of one industry into another tends to raise overall costs.

3. Business firms should take advantage of the cost savings achieved through mass production, known to economists as economies of scale. For this reason big business may be socially necessary for economic efficiency. Note, however, that firms can become so large that they become less efficient. (The classic illustrations of this possibility are the big three automobile manufactures and big banks here in the USA.)

Price minimization requires not only that resource costs be minimized but also that profit margins be the socially necessary minimum. Firms must be allowed to earn enough profit to keep entrepreneurs—owners and managers—in business in the long run. Economists call this normal profit. Things that tend to raise profits above these normal levels, such as monopoly power and much government regulation, cause economic inefficiency.

ECONOMIC SECURITY

Our economic security objective has two dimensions: First, every member of society should be assured of a minimum standard of living in order to eliminate the extremes of poverty. This minimum income level needed to eliminate poverty is determined by the very nature of society. An individual must have a certain minimum level of vitality, appearance, protection and training in order to get respectable employment, to be socially acceptable to others, to know what is going on in society, and to live rather than exist. (This "poverty level of income" is higher in this country than in most other nations.)

Second, every member of society should be protected from the various contingencies which can adversely affect accustomed standards of living. Death, disability and sickness not only reduce income but also increase costs. Becoming unemployed and even unemployable because of sickness or a disability will dramatically reduce income but it also can increase costs. Because the proportion of people affected by each such contingency is predictable for society as a whole, and since most people take about the same risk, the insurance principle of spreading risk can be applied. Hence, social insurance is used extensively to protect economic security. How far society wants to go with this concept is controversial. Most advanced economies have accepted social responsibility for the provision of such services as medical care and disability insurance to most members of society.

ECONOMIC FREEDOM

Economists believe that people with different tastes and preferences should be free to pursue their own self-interest. Nobody should be able to impose his or her values and preferences on others. Hence, a system of individual or private decision-making is socially desirable as an objective in itself. Of course, there are social limits to free decision-making. Nevertheless, people should be free to make decisions for themselves as long as those decisions do not impose significant costs on others. Of course, there are various restraints on economic freedom:
- social norms that inhibit our behavior;
- laws and regulations imposed by governments;
- the accumulation of economic power;
- deference to those with wealth; and
- the distortion of our thinking caused by the conditioning of our values by tradition, religion, education and advertising.

LIBERALS VERSUS CONSERVATIVES

While we have social and international objectives as well, very few Americans would disagree with any of our economic objectives. Virtually nothing is omitted. In principle, little is controversial. Where we run into difficulty is with our priorities among these objectives. In broad terms people who are more liberal tend to give the highest priority to economic security. Those who are more conservative usually give preference to economic freedom and economic efficiency.

It is within each individual goal category that major disagreements occur:

- Within the economic stability objective, conservatives are more concerned about price stability and combating inflation then liberals, who are more interested in full employment, especially of human resources.

- Within the economic growth objective, conservatives tend to be more interested in long-term growth rates and protection of our existing way of life. Liberals are usually more concerned with instant gratification, environmental concerns, and income distribution issues.

- It is within the economic efficiency objective that some of the greatest disparities occur. For example, conservatives are far more willing that liberals to give the lower income groups subsidies or welfare benefits in cash, trusting the relatively poor to act in their own best self-interest. Liberals usually want to dole out specific benefits such as food stamps and rent subsidies. Conservatives are more supportive of technological change, big business and higher profits. Liberals are far more concerned about discrimination issues.

- Within the economic security objective, liberals would define the poverty level—the income below which people are poor—at a higher income level than conservatives would. Liberals seem to believe that everyone should be protected from all contingencies so that our society becomes virtually risk free. Conservatives are much more interested in protecting society against unpredictable contingencies. The classic illustration is medical care where liberals prefer to have social insurance for all medical treatment while conservatives would tend to prefer to limit coverage to major medical expenses.

- Within the economic freedom objective, liberals tend to be more supportive of legal limits, government regulation, restrictions on monopoly power, social costs, and upper limits on wealth. Conservatives are far more willing to accept private decision-making without many social restrictions and involvement by the public sector.

One final note must be added to our discussion of economic objectives. There is no truth, no right, no wrong! We differ in what we believe society should strive to achieve and how society should go about doing so. When we deal with what we should do, the discussion enters the realm of politics and leaves that of economics. The economist's opinion is no better than the politician's opinion or the reader's opinion. In short, your opinion is as good as mine!

FOOTNOTES

1 Jim DeMint and J. David Woodard; "Why We Whisper: Restoring Our Right to Say It's Wrong"; Rowman & Littlefield Publishers, Inc.; 2008; p. 16

2 Michael Gerson; "Too Much Ideology, Not Enough Wonkery"; Arizona Republic, 1/19/2012, p. B7)

3 Robert J. Samuelson; Arizona Republic, 12/27/11, p. B9

9

EVALUATIONS

This chapter is divided into four sections. The first two are critiques of liberalism and conservatism as political philosophies, trying to be as objective and impartial as possible by stating the case precisely point by point. Then there is a whimsical section of "fun" things from the internet---"fables" that have a moral to them. The final section is a short personal statement on the essential difference between liberals and conservatives.

A CRITIQUE OF LIBERALISM

Our critique of American liberalism will be in three parts. The first will examine two fundamental problems anyone faces when trying to evaluate liberalism in general. The second will take a neutral and somewhat philosophical point of view toward American liberalism, offering up a series of seven of the major criticisms of liberalism. The third will look at liberalism in this country from a conservative viewpoint, looking at why conservatives are so vehemently opposed to liberal thinking and liberal public policies.

FUNDAMENTAL PROBLEMS

#1—NEBULOUS NATURE. The basic difficulty we face when trying to evaluate liberalism is that it is such a nebulous and undefinable phenomenon. It is always moving away from something toward something else. This raises four simple questions with difficult answers:

1. What is it moving away from? In my opinion, it is moving away from our past and our present. In short, it is never satisfied with where American society has been or currently is.

2. What is it moving toward? In my opinion, it is moving toward a vague and ambiguous utopia that even its leading proponents are unable or unwilling to define.

3. What is it seeking? In my opinion, it is seeking more of everything and anything. To be as precise as possible, its quest is for more freedom, more equality, more justice, more security, and more government.

4. What is the process? In my opinion, liberalism has no specific agenda. It is like floodwaters seeking out the weakest point in a levee system in order to break through its restraining barriers, and then always flowing downhill toward the lowest point.

In short, liberalism takes whatever it can whenever it can. It seizes targets of opportunity with little concern for specific priorities.

> Long ago, Samuel Gompers was a union leader who founded the American Federation of Labor (AFL), the federation of craft-oriented unions. When testifying before a Congressional hearing on the labor movement, he was asked what organized labor wanted. His response was simply, "More!" When asked what labor wanted after it had more, he replied, "More!" When finally asked what the ultimate objective of organized labor was, he once again replied, "More!" This true story is a beautiful description not only of the labor movement but also of liberalism. The motto and operational objective of liberalism could easily be put in Gompers' famous quotation: "We want more, and when it becomes more, we shall still want more. And we shall never cease to demand more."

#2—**EXTREMISM.** America was founded as a liberal nation. Throughout its history, America has steadfastly remained a liberal nation. America today is a liberal nation. America will remain a liberal nation for the foreseeable future. Yet at any given point in time, America seems to be a conservative nation. The big picture is one of liberalism; the local scene in that picture is usually but not always one of conservatism. Just look back at history. America was founded as a free and liberal nation escaping the tyranny of the church and aristocracy in Europe. From the start, America had an economy based on capitalism, free markets and free trade. America was the first major nation to guarantee its citizens freedom of speech, assembly and the press. America has used its industrial strength and young men to protect democracy elsewhere in World Wars I and II as well as the Cold War.

After winning World War II, America rebuilt its former enemies—Japan and Germany—with the Marshall Plan; no other nation in all of history has treated its enemies that well. America was responsible for founding the world's major international organizations—the League of Nations after World War I (although the Senate refused to go along), United Nations, International Monetary Fund, World Bank, etc., after World War II. America established a safety net of Social Security, Medicare, Medicaid and other programs for its less fortunate citizens. America has stood alone right from the beginning in its support of Israel and Jewry—the only democracy in the Near East. Americans believe in helping others facing disaster—our own people (Katrina) and foreigners (tsunamis, earthquakes and floods). America is open to new ideas and new immigrants. America is well known for its charitable giving, both domestically and abroad.

In sum, we can all be proud to say that America is a liberal nation. We are all liberals now. We can criticize some aspects of liberalism in the here and now, and I am among the first to be quite critical. But just look at what liberalism has wrought in the long run. America is a bright and shining light for the world and none of us should ever forget that. Yes, we are all liberals now and that is a good thing.

So what is the problem? There is little that is wrong with liberalism. It's liberals that create difficulties for us. Liberalism is okay, but liberals always go to extremes. There are two classic illustrations of this point. The first is the liberal quest for freedom which has gone so far as to give society problems with drugs, sexual promiscuity, pornography, vulgarity, etc. The second is the liberal quest for equality which has gone from equality in the law and equal economic opportunity, both of which are acceptable to most Americans, to equality of economic and social outcomes, which cannot be achieved without destroying personal freedom and economic incentives. A historically important example is the separation of church and state, pushed to its limits by a liberal judiciary, whereby things have gone so far that we cannot even talk about Christmas celebrations. A very current illustration would be gay rights, where many of us feel that allowing gays to have more legal rights toward each other is just fine so long as they don't call it marriage, but the gay movement, like most other liberal movements before it, always wants to push the envelope.

The bottom line is simply that having liberalism define the long-run general nature of our society is acceptable to virtually all of us. But liberalism as a short-term activist movement is not. We like where we are as a society but don't necessarily like where we seem to be going. There is a contradiction here and it is probably impossible to reconcile these statements. It may just come down to the pace of change. Liberals are unhappy with where we are, want things to change, and feel that the quicker the better. The rest of us are happy with where we are and are willing to savor the moment.

THE MAJOR CRITICISMS

#1—THE INHERENT CONFLICT. Most people see American liberalism as having two primary objectives: freedom and equality. But there is a conflict between the two of them. Freedom allows people to follow different paths and they become unequal in the process. To achieve equality, especially equality of outcomes, requires social coercion and market interference by a strong government that destroys freedom. So:
* Freedom means less equality.
* Equality means less freedom.

Hence, liberalism cannot achieve both freedom and equality across the board. It must keep the two in separate domains. Liberalism in the US has compromised its fundamental principles by limiting its quest for freedom to the social realm and its pursuit of equality to the economic and political realms. As a result, there is a continuing tension within liberalism among social, economic and political objectives.

#2—THE VIRTUE PROBLEM. To be successful, a liberal society needs leadership with what is called "virtue"—a combination of competence and character. To obtain such leadership, liberalism historically has relied on society's nongovernmental institutions—families, neighborhoods, churches, schools, unions, charitable organizations, social clubs, and voluntary civic associations. It is from such foundations that men and women of competence and character gain experience as leaders. Unfortunately, liberalism tends to promote its primary objectives of freedom and equality for the individual in ways that weaken all these social institutions. So liberalism creates conditions in which developing the needed virtues is unlikely on a large scale. The long-term viability of a liberal society comes into question unless its families, schools, churches, and civic organizations are strengthened. Sadly, however, the liberal tendency is to weaken our nongovernmental institutions rather than strengthen them. So liberalism tends to destroy what it needs.

#3—DISTRUST OF FREE ENTERPRISE. In principle, liberals believe in capitalism and a free market economy. In practice, they are overly concerned about the problems associated with capitalism: instability, inequality, insecurity and the inefficiencies associated with market power and social costs (negative externalities such as pollution). Because of these misgivings, they want government to be heavily involved in private decision-making and the regulation of business. All economists believe that some such involvement and regulation is absolutely necessary, but many feel that it goes too far under liberalism. In effect, many of our large business firms have become quasi-public enterprises, much like public utilities. This is a bigger problem in Europe and other socialist-leaning countries than it is in America, but even here it is already a problem and becoming steadily worse under the Democratic administration of Barack Obama. The result is a reluctance of business leaders to expand their enterprises and invest in our economy, holding down the rates of employment and economic growth.

> It is interesting to note that the rest of the world is deregulating to become more like the United States, while we are increasing regulation to become more like everyone else.

Four broad observations about our free-market economy seem appropriate here:

- Most Americans accept the concept of self-interest for themselves but are suspicious of the self-interest of others.
- American society places heavy burdens on business, making it a vehicle to attain such social objectives as environmental protection and personal security.

- Liberal politicians and the Democratic Party would prefer to see all businesses and especially large corporations function as regulated public utilities.
- It doesn't take communism or socialism to weaken or destroy capitalism and free enterprise; liberalism seems to do a pretty good job of doing that.

#4—HOSTILITY TO RELIGION. Liberalism has attacked religion and successfully promoted its long-term decline in America. The process has been multifaceted. Our liberal, intellectual elites, either indifferent or hostile to religion, have succeeded in removing religion from most social debate. Our liberal judiciary has used the First Amendment to impose a barrier between religion and government. Our liberal press either ignores religion completely, treats it with disdain, or sees it as a threat to modernity and social progress. Our liberal educational establishment has promoted modern science as the solution to all of our difficulties—physical, social, political and ethical—treating religion as meaningless and primitive superstition with nothing important to say about society's problems. The radicals in the feminist and gay liberation movements have vehemently opposed religion because of its perceived male domination, adherence to strict traditional beliefs, and authoritative hierarchical structure. Many of our religious institutions have moved to the left, trying to remain relevant by changing with the times in order to maintain membership. Religious services and sermons are increasingly about modern concepts of love, kindness, and eternal life, rather than traditional beliefs in sin, virtue, salvation and damnation. It is no coincidence that the declines of American culture and morality have taken place at the same time as the decline of American religion. It has always been religion that set American standards for personal conduct—such things as civility, self-restraint and industry—the basis of our morality. In short, liberalism has been a major contributor to the decline of American culture and American morality, raising a serious question about the future viability of our way of life and society.

#5—MORAL AND CULTURAL DECLINE. Closely related to liberalism's hostility toward religion is the steady erosion of morality and culture in America. The signs are everywhere. The deterioration of the family can be seen in the growing prevalence of divorce, the rapidly rising number of single parents, and the trend toward cohabitation without marriage. The deterioration of individual behavior can be seen in growing sexual promiscuity, the rising number of out-of-wedlock births, the growth of the drug culture, pornography, and increasing crime and violence throughout our society. The deterioration of education can be seen in the declining performance of American students relative to students abroad, growing violence in our schools, and the need for remedial classes to teach basic writing and mathematical skills in our universities. The deterioration of the English language can be seen in its growing vulgarity. The deterioration of entertainment can be seen in its growing reliance on sex, brutality and obscenity as entertainers seek authenticity by attacking cultural standards. And the list goes on.

We can place most of the blame, if not all, on liberalism. Its emphasis on freedom for the individual has turned into behavioral license and sensual hedonism. Its support for the feminist and gay rights movements has been a major factor in the weakening of the family in America. Its attack on religion has virtually destroyed the moral standards that helped make this country great. Its judicial rulings have not only weakened the limitations on individual behavior so as to make them almost nonexistent, but also made it more difficult and time-consuming to apprehend and punish criminals. Its control of most of the media has ensured that its point of view dominates social and political discussion. Its takeover of higher education has guaranteed that each succeeding generation of young people will become more radical and liberated. And the list goes on.

In America, the combination of affluence and the reduced time and effort required for work brings with it boredom and a life increasingly centered on consumption and entertainment. Our sensations must be steadily intensified to prevent boredom. Modern technology—especially computers, television and hand-held devices—has stepped in with two important results:

- Entertainment has become more sensual, sexual, and violent.
- We have become obsessed with personal convenience above everything else, making us all impatient with anything–such as religion, morality and the law–which interferes with our personal convenience.

#6—MOVEMENT LIBERALISM. Just because someone seems to be a fervent advocate of a cause does not necessarily mean that cause is his or her primary consideration. This is especially true of the liberal elite. The classic case, but not the only one, is environmentalism. Economists can show us how to achieve clean air and water at reasonable cost. However, this is not what fanatic environmentalists want. Reducing air and water pollution is really only a means to an end. What environmentalists really want is to change modern industrial society and its technology. They are hostile to a market economy where the wishes of the majority of common people determine what is to be produced. They want the authority to create and control our economic system and environment—not just the physical ecology but also the social environment—in a way that pleases them and meets their standards. You can be certain that the society environmentalists want will be one that they, the liberal elite, can control to the exclusion of the wishes of the rest of us. All too often, movement liberals have a hidden agenda. And that agenda typically involves a complete overhaul and repudiation of our free enterprise system. What you see is not what you get.

There is a second problem with movement liberalism. Each and every movement wants to protect its favored group from any form of physical suffering or mental anguish. This has been true for each movement advocating special rights for its group—women, blacks, Hispanics, gays, illegal immigrants, and even animals. Each group has come to be seen as victims of social injustice deserving special treatment and government protection. We have become a nation of victims. The only category excluded from this process seemingly is white males; they are the oppressors.

#7—CIVIC ASSOCIATIONS. Closely related to the virtue problem, liberalism has been a major factor in causing the decline of and changes in our civic associations, from the Lions Club and Boy Scouts of America to local country clubs, churches, and nonprofit associations. There are various reasons:

- Liberalism has shifted society's focus from the community to the individual, making civic organizations less needed and less relevant to people.
- With the advent of the Great Society, voluntary organizations have increasingly provided social services funded by the federal government.

Membership dues and fund raising have become less of a problem, but close personal ties have also been lost in the process.

- Anti-discrimination laws have been liberally interpreted to control who must be allowed into many civic organizations, making members less homogeneous and thus less likely to remain focused on the associations' original purposes. (Many all-male organizations have been forced to admit women, changing their very nature. Young girls have been allowed to join boy's sports teams, even such contact sports as football.) Rather than allowing a diversity of various kinds of associations, liberalism seeks to attain membership diversity within each and every individual association. The result is that our civic associations have become less distinctive and more uniform.

SPECIFIC COMPLAINTS

Many people—conservatives, moderates and some liberals—are critical of liberalism in general or of specific aspects of liberalism that they dislike. Yet they have never thought in such abstract terms as the nebulous nature of liberalism, as liberalism being okay but liberals too extreme, as there being an inherent conflict between freedom and equality, or as there being a virtue problem. Yet these people have specific complaints against liberalism and liberals. What follows is a simple laundry list of the major criticisms of liberalism and liberals made by people of diverse political positions, but especially by those of us who are relatively conservative:

- Liberals always seek utopian solutions for economic, social and political problems. They regularly underestimate the difficulties not only of coming up with good policies but also of administering them. They overpromise results in an optimistic belief that they can solve any problem. They generally ignore or underestimate the side effects, almost always negative, of their policy proposals.

- Liberals always see government as the solution to virtually any problem. They always ignore the fact that many of society's problems are caused by faulty government policies. They always ignore the possibility of there being private solutions to our major socioeconomic problems. Unfortunately, the public sector does very few things nearly as well or as inexpensively as the private sector.

- Liberals always favor a large and growing public sector. They want to give more power to government. They favor European-style socialism to American-style capitalism. Their operational objective seems to be to increase the power of government to do what it thinks best for the people. Yet it is difficult not only to design and implement policies that are best for the masses but also to know what is truly best for them.

- Liberals always seek to consolidate power rather than to diffuse power. When seeking to solve problems they always favor state governments over local governments, the federal government over state governments, and international governing institutions over national governments. For many, world government is their ultimate, utopian objective.

- Liberals always see too much good in people and ignore the dark side of human nature. They always underestimate the willingness and ability of people to take advantage of the largesse of the public sector. As a result, they do not devote enough attention and resources to the administration and enforcement of public policy, especially when some form of handout is involved.

- Liberals always see morality as being relative rather than absolute, personal rather than social, local rather than universal, and subjective rather than objective. They have presided over a steady decline of this country's ethical standards and morality. As a result, they have always been weak on crime, cheating in school, sexual promiscuity, unwed mothers, the drug problem, and the like.

- Liberals always believe that the present situation can be improved. They are thus optimistic about the future, their own ability to influence it, and the possibilities of change. They will always choose reform over stability and experimentation over continuity. They always prefer rapid over gradual and extensive over incremental change.

- Liberalism has made America into a nation of dependents. This is true of such groups as the poor, the aged, the sick, the disabled, the single parent and the unemployed. It is also true of those with good income— farmers, scientists and academics. It is even true of many of our large corporations—in banking, in finance, in manufacturing and in energy. The majority of us receive some form of payment or personal benefit directly from the government. Handouts and subsidies are everywhere, and nobody wants to give up their own.

- Liberalism has seemingly accepted as a basic right the position that almost anything that people need to live the good life should be made readily available by society and if necessary financed by the government. This concept of having the public sector meeting everyone's basic needs has gone far beyond having society provide everyone with a safety net protecting people against such contingencies as disability, sickness, aging, unemployment, etc. The truth is, however, that it is not the function of government to make us all happy, but rather to enable most of us to make ourselves happy.

- Modern liberalism has sought to make America a risk-free society. We have greater personal security than any society in all history. Yet we have become increasingly apprehensive about our lives. We want to be totally insulated from risk. Security is liberalism's religion. We demand security not only from major difficulties, but also from minor inconveniences. Thus, health insurance covers not only the cost of major surgery and prolonged hospitalization, but also the charges for regular medical checkups and every pill we take. Security and freedom from risk have become another right.

- Liberals always support higher tax rates on high-income earners even if that doesn't increase the total taxes the rich pay. The effect is not to help the poor but rather to pull down the rich. The liberal approach is to reduce inequality by bringing the more fortunate down rather than by bringing the less fortunate up. This is the liberal politics of envy. Envy is not just about inequality; it is also about who is rich. The rich businessman is resented; the rich athlete or entertainer is not. In essence, liberals dislike the rich, the successful, and the businessman. And when someone is all three, oh boy!

A CRITIQUE OF CONSERVATISM

Conservatives are extremely disappointed with what is currently going on in American politics. They feel that the Republican Party has failed them miserably. Their problem—the source of frustration—is that they have no reasonable alternative for a political home. Conservatism can be criticized in terms of political ideology; the Republican Party in terms of practical politics. We will examine seven major concerns about American conservatism and the Republican Party.

#1—THE FAILURES

Modern conservatism has been politically successful in winning elections, but it must be judged to be an abject failure. It has failed to achieve all three of its major objectives:

- Conservatives have failed to reverse or even slow the growth of the liberal welfare state.
- Conservatives have failed to reverse or even slow the growth of government spending and regulation of the private economy.
- Conservatives have failed to reverse or even slow society's moral decay.

#2—THE ECONOMICS PLATFORM

Conservatives always campaign by promising to reduce income-tax rates, government regulation of the private economy, and the size of government. There are definite problems with this approach to political campaigning. Let's look first at tax reduction as a political issue and public policy:

- After repeated tax reductions, most Americans now pay relatively little in income taxes. About half the adult population pays no income taxes at all. So taxes are not that big an issue with most people.
- While many of our society's problems relate directly back to the federal government and its programs, few of them can be fixed or even reduced by cutting taxes and reducing regulation.
- With this country having huge fiscal deficits, the time of across-the-board tax reductions for the middle class is over.
- If taxes are to be a part of solving current problems, we need to use taxes to increase positive incentives on the supply side far more than to raise private spending on the demand side.

Looking next at deregulation, we can agree on the need for less government control of small business in general and perhaps some specific areas of control for all business, such as labor relations and worker dismissal rules. However, there are at least two areas where deregulation has done far more harm than good—public utilities and large financial institutions. In the case of public utilities, there are two problems: First, with deregulation, the large corporations that supply electricity, water, natural gas, gasoline and the internet have been cutting back on investment and modernization, allowing the infrastructure on which modern life and our economy depend to be hollowed out. We are falling behind our foreign competitors in infrastructure. Second, and perhaps even more important, the maintenance of our privately-owned facilities has deteriorated, with adverse implications for safety and continuity of service. (The deplorable state of our pipelines and electrical transmission is well known. Natural disasters like Sandy sure make that obvious.)

As for financial deregulation, all we need to say is that it played a major part in the financial debacle and great recession of 2007 and 2008. Because of a lack of government control and industry self-discipline, most large financial institutions took on far too much risk and minimized their overall capitalization. When large numbers of mortgages went into default and the value of asset portfolios declined, many large institutions failed and took the entire economy down with them. Conservatives, nevertheless, continue to oppose financial regulation and want to continue with more deregulation, which has seemingly done far more harm then good. They haven't learned a thing from recent history.

The problem with reducing the size of the federal government is that the vast majority of federal spending goes to defense, health care, Social Security, and interest on the national debt. Everything else—what makes up nondefense discretionary spending—comes to only 12% of the budget. But the Republicans are never willing to specify which items within that eighth of the budget they propose to cut for fear of alienating large groups of voters.

In short, conservative politics offers simple and short-sighted solutions from the past to deal with the complex and long-term problems of the present and future. Conservatives are all too prone to beating a dead horse.

#3—LACK OF VISION

Conservatives have a definite vision problem. We all know what conservatives are against, namely whatever liberals are for: equality, freedom from social restraints (multiculturalism and behavioral license), big government (the welfare state), and government regulation and control of the private economy. But what are conservatives for? What is the conservative program? And how are they going to get their program enacted? In the presidential campaign of 2012, most of us knew what President Barack Obama was for, but had little knowledge of what Governor Mitt Romney was proposing as an alternative. Is the conservative-Republican agenda to just say no? Is the idea to just clean up the mess being left by the liberal-Democrats? Are the conservatives just saying that they can and will manage the liberal program better than the liberals can and will run it?

#4—MOVEMENT CONSERVATISM

The Republican Party is almost completely dominated by movement conservatism—a rigid and doctrinaire ideology of the right. This doctrine of extremism encompasses four prongs:

- supporting capitalism, free markets and the deregulation of the economy;
- supporting low taxation and small government;
- supporting an aggressive and unilateral foreign policy backed by large military forces; and
- fighting the culture wars against liberal social policies.

These were the hallmark beliefs of the eight years of the George W. Bush presidency, and all four must be judged as failures at best and disasters at worst, especially in how they resulted in the repudiation of the Republican Party in the 2008 election. Yet little, if anything, changed in the run-up to the 2012 election. The extreme doctrines of movement conservatism still dominate the Republican Party. Oddly enough, Ronald Reagan is revered by conservatives, but his administration rejected the extreme for the center, purity for pragmatism, and the conservative dream for reality. Reagan was conservative but not a fanatic, and as a result, he was politically successful. Unfortunately, that lesson has been lost on those that followed him.

Richard Nixon was also a conservative Republican president, but he was more pragmatic than ideological—more concerned with practical results than with theories and principles. He will always be remembered for opening the door for relations with China and will go down in history as an effective president, even though there was a dark side to his time in office.

#5—GOVERNANCE

Since conservatives don't believe in government, they are not very good at governing. Their ideology keeps getting in the way of their performance. Just ask yourself questions like these about conservatives and you will see the problem:

- How can you effectively stabilize the economy and prevent business cycles when (1) you believe that the federal budget should always be balanced, which makes fiscal policy impotent and in fact procyclical rather than countercyclical; and (2) you don't trust the Federal Reserve Board or its conduct of monetary policy, and in fact embrace libertarians who want to eliminate the Fed?
- How can you effectively regulate the private sector when you vehemently support laissez faire and actively dislike all forms of regulation and government bureaucracy?
- How can you efficiently run the various social welfare programs that help those who are relatively less well off when you believe that (1) many of the poor create their own problems and thus deserve to be poor; and (2) social welfare programs create far more problems than they prevent or cure?
- How can you effectively run our vast array of environmental programs when you (1) don't trust scientists or their scientific evidence; and (2) believe that global warming is a monumental hoax perpetrated by liberal extremists and do-gooders?

In short, because conservatives dislike government and so many public policies, they are ineffective in making use of them. They are far more effective as an opposition party, when they can argue against public policy, than as the party in power, when they are forced to formulate public policy.

Proof positive of this position is seen in two major things that happened during George W. Bush's administration. First, when hurricane Katrina hit New Orleans and the surrounding area so very hard, the Bush administration wanted to leave the problem in the hands of authorities originally at the local level and then at the state level. Federal involvement was inadequate and belated. Second, when the Bush administration made the fateful decision to undertake military intervention in first Afghanistan and then Iraq, their planning for war was meticulous and effective, but they forgot to think ahead as to what was to happen after victory was achieved. As a result, in both countries, we won the war and lost the peace.

#6—RHETORIC: ALL HAT, NO CATTLE

Conservatives seemingly don't believe their own rhetoric. After eight years of criticizing Bill Clinton and his Democratic administration, Republican conservatives won control of the presidency and both houses in Washington. They finally had the power to put the conservative program into effect. But what did they do? Rather than cut back on liberal social-welfare programs, they passed the first new social-welfare program (prescription benefits for seniors) in over a quarter of a century. Rather than show fiscal discipline, they cut income taxes and increased government spending across the board, creating a huge fiscal deficit that has continued to plague us to this day. Simply stated, conservatives don't put their money where their mouth is. As Bush's Texans would say, they are all hat and no cattle.

> It has been said that the motto of the Democratic Party is "tax, tax, tax, spend, spend, spend, elect, elect, elect." Could we now say that the motto for the Republican Party is "taxcut, taxcut, taxcut, spend, spend, spend, elect, elect, elect?" Republicans have proven themselves to be no better than Democrats. Both are just politicians out to reward their friends and supporters with little, if any, regard for what society as a whole wants and needs.

#7—EXCLUSION

The conservative Republican Party has become increasingly exclusive. It gets its support more from men than from women, more from whites than from Latinos and African-Americans, more from the religious than from nonbelievers, more from higher-income groups than from lower-income groups, more from the old than from the young, and more from the poorly educated than from the well-educated. It has alienated women because of its views on abortion, rape and equal pay. It has alienated Hispanics because of its views on immigration. It has alienated African Americans because of its views on transfer payments, affirmative action, and race relations in general. It has alienated the religious because of not only its views on the social and cultural issues, but also its disdain for religion and morality. It has alienated low-income voters because of its open hostility toward those who pay few income taxes but receive transfers and benefits from the government. It has alienated the young because it has not accepted our evolving culture of permissiveness and tolerance. It has alienated the educated because of its contempt for scientific evidence, academia, and the intelligentsia.

In 2012, the conservative Republican Party looked more and more like a club for old white men. And the demographic trends are against it as Latinos and former immigrants become a larger proportion of the voting population. Such exclusiveness could well be the Achilles heel of conservatism and the Republican Party.

WHAT WAS FOUND ON THE INTERNET

We all receive interesting things from our friends via E-mail. I thought four particular items relevant to our discussion. I don't know who wrote them, but they are interesting and worthwhile.

HOW CAN YOU CATCH WILD PIGS?

You catch wild pigs by finding a suitable place in the woods and putting corn on the ground. The pigs find it and begin to come everyday to eat the free corn. When they are used to coming every day, you put a fence down one side of the place where they are used to coming. When they get used to the fence, they begin to eat the corn again and you put up another side of the fence. They get used to that and start to eat again. You continue until you have all four sides of the fence up with a gate in the last side. The pigs, which are used to the free corn, start to come through the gate to eat that free corn again. You then slam the gate on them and catch the whole herd. Suddenly the wild pigs have lost their freedom. They run around and around inside the fence, but they are caught. Soon they go back to eating the free corn. They are so used to it that they have forgotten how to forage in the woods for themselves, so they accept their captivity.

This is exactly what many of us see happening in America. The government keeps spreading the free corn out in the form of its various programs of subsidies, handouts and benefits coupled with tax exemptions, credits and cuts, while we continually lose our freedoms, just a little at a time.

If you see all of this wonderful government "help" as a problem confronting the future of democracy in America, you are probably a conservative. If you think the free ride is essential to your way of life, then you are probably a liberal. But God help you when the gate slams shut because there is no such thing as a free lunch.

IRONY IN GOVERNMENT

On Tuesday, February 28, 2012, the SNAP/Food Stamp Program, administered by the United States Department of Agriculture, announced that it was pleased to be distributing the greatest amount of free meals and food stamps ever. Meanwhile, the National Park Service, administered by the United States Department of the Interior, was telling the public: "Please Do Not Feed the Animals." This is because the animals may grow dependent on handouts and not learn to take care of themselves.

This ends today's lesson on irony in government.

A FABLE: BAR STOOL ECONOMICS

Every day, ten men go out for beers and the bill for all ten comes to $100. If they paid their bill the way we pay our taxes, it would go something like this:
- The first four men (the poorest) would pay nothing.
- The fifth would pay $1.
- The sixth would pay $3.
- The seventh would pay $7.

- The eighth would pay $12.
- The ninth would pay $18.
- The tenth man (the richest) would pay $59.

So, that's what they decided to do. The ten men drank in the bar every day and seemed quite happy with the arrangement.

Then, one day, the owner threw them a curve. "Since you are all such good customers," he said, "I'm going to reduce the cost of your daily beer by $20." Drinks for the ten now cost just $80. The group still wanted to pay their bill the way we pay our taxes so the first four men were unaffected. They would still drink for free. But what about the other six men—the paying customers? How could they divide the $20 windfall so that everyone would get his 'fair share?' They realized that $20 divided by six is $3.33. But if they subtracted that from everybody's share, then the fifth and sixth men would each end up being paid to drink their beer. So, the bar owner suggested a plan to reduce each man's bill, and he worked out the amounts each should pay. And so:

- The fifth man, like the first four, now paid nothing (100% savings).
- The sixth now paid $2 instead of $3 (33% savings).
- The seventh now paid $5 instead of $7 (28% savings).
- The eighth now paid $9 instead of $12 (25% savings).
- The ninth now paid $14 instead of $18 (22% savings).
- The tenth now paid $49 instead of $59 (16% savings).

Note that the tenth man got the smallest percentage reduction and now paid 61.25% of the total bill, where he previously paid 59% of the bill. Note also that each of the six was better off than before. And the first four continued to drink for free.

Once outside the restaurant, the men began to compare their savings. "I only got a dollar discount from the $20 declared the sixth man. He pointed to the tenth man, "but he got $10!" "Yeah, that's right," exclaimed the fifth man. "I only saved a dollar, too. It's unfair that he got ten times more than I!" "That's true!!" shouted the seventh man. "Why should he get $10 back when I got only two? The wealthy get all the breaks!" "Wait a minute," yelled the first four men in unison. "We didn't get anything at all. The whole system exploits the poor!" The nine men surrounded the tenth and beat him up.

The next night the tenth man didn't show up for drinks, so the nine sat down and had beers without him. But when it came time to pay the bill, they discovered something important. They didn't have enough money between all of them for even half of the bill!

And that is how our tax system works. The people who pay the highest taxes get the most benefit from a tax reduction. Tax them too much, attack them for being wealthy, and they just may not show up anymore. In fact, they might start drinking overseas where the atmosphere is somewhat friendlier.

For those who understand, no explanation is needed. For those who do not understand, no explanation is possible.

THE FABLE OF THE NIGHT WATCHMAN

Once upon a time the government had a vast military scrap yard in the middle of the California desert. The Chairman of the Congressional Oversight Committee worried that someone may steal from it at night. So they created a night watchman position and hired a person for the job. Then the Chairman asked how the watchman could do his job without proper instruction. So they created a planning department and hired two people, one person to write the instructions, and one person to do time studies. Then the Chairman asked how we will know the night watchman is doing his tasks correctly. So they created a quality control department and hired two people. One was to do the studies and one was to write the reports. Then the Chairman asked how all these people are going to get paid. So they created positions for a time keeper and payroll officer, and then hired two people. Then the chairman asked who would be accountable for all of these people. So they created an administrative section and hired three people—an administrative officer, assistant administrative officer, and a legal secretary. A year later, the Chairman noted that this command had been in operation for a year but was $900,000 over budget and had to cut back. So they laid-off the night watchman.

This fable sounds pretty ridiculous, doesn't it? Perhaps! Does anybody remember the reason given for the establishment of the Department of Energy during the Carter administration? We've spent several hundred billion dollars in support of the Department of Energy, which was instituted on 8/04/1977, to reduce our dependence on foreign oil. And now, 35 years later, the budget for the Department of Energy is over $24 billion per year. It has 16,000 federal employees and about 100,000 contract employees. And just look at how effective a job the Department of Energy has done. Thirty-five years ago 30% of our oil consumption was foreign imports. Today 70% of our oil consumption is foreign imports.

THE BOTTOM LINE

Students used to ask me what the major difference is between liberals and conservatives. The best I could do to deal with this question was to narrow my answer to four simple sentences:

- Liberals believe that if we take care of the short run, the long run will take care of itself; while conservatives believe that if we take care of the long run, the short run will take care of itself.
- Liberals believe that government is the solution to most economic and social problems; while conservatives believe that government (especially liberal public policy) is the cause of most economic and social problems.
- Liberals believe that morality and moral standards are relative to and different for each society; while conservatives believe that morality and moral standards are absolute and unchanging for all societies.
- Liberals seek freedom in the social sphere but accept coercion in the economic realm, while conservatives do the opposite, seeking freedom in the economy and accepting coercion in society.

10

ECONOMIC CONSERVATISM

Most conservatives and many liberals are well familiar with the postulates of modern conservatism discussed in the fifth chapter. Few people, no matter what their political and philosophical persuasion, are familiar with many of the postulates of economic conservatism that follow. There are twelve of them. Some of the postulates will find most economists agreeing with them. Some are more controversial and will find greater disagreement.

#1—STABILITY

The markets for most goods and services are inherently stable. The markets for most assets, especially financial assets, real estate and some commodities with futures markets, are inherently unstable. The overall economy, which includes both stable and unstable sectors, lies somewhere between but definitely leans toward stability. Let's look at these three related statements individually.

The markets for most goods and services are inherently stable. To see why, let's look at a hypothetical example. Suppose scientists announce that eating more pork is good for us and can extend our lifespan a couple of years. The demand for pork will clearly rise, causing the price of pork to increase. Pig farmers will respond by raising more pigs and producing more pork. Of course, this takes time but eventually the supply of pork will rise to meet the increase in demand. The quantity of pork being produced and eaten will rise. The price of pork will rise significantly at first but gradually fall again to approximately where it was before the announcement. What happens is that a change in demand eventually causes an offsetting change in supply, stabilizing the price. We can say that the market for pork is stable—inherently stable. This is true for the markets for most goods and services.

The markets for most assets, especially financial assets, real estate and some commodities with futures markets, are inherently unstable. Let's use a real-world example to see why. In the 1990s, the technical sector of the economy started booming. The demand for and price of tech stocks started to rise. The rising price of tech stocks caused more and more people to jump on the bandwagon to buy more and more stocks. Those who were already holding such stocks would not sell; so the supply of tech stocks in the marketplace dried up. The increase in demand and reduction in supply drove stock prices higher. Expecting even higher prices, this caused a further speculative increase in demand and reduction in supply, just the opposite of what happens in stable markets. The prices of these stocks rose.... and rose.....and rose. Eventually the prices of tech stocks got to ridiculous levels that could not be sustained. The market crashed and everything went into reverse, so stock prices fell precipitously, as much as 90% from their highs.

When a change in demand causes a further change in demand in the same direction, a market is said to be unstable and has a boom-and-bust tendency leading periodically to wild speculative price increases followed by catastrophic crashes. This is precisely what happened to the housing market in the following decade—a long period of rising home prices to unprecedented levels followed by the collapse of the real estate market, triggering the Great Recession beginning in 2008.

There is a sad dimension to this example. I knew of people who correctly forecast the boom in tech stocks. They rode the market all the way to the top, becoming wealthy in the process. All they had to do to live a life of luxury was sell. But they didn't. Being very conservative and hating government as much as they do, they were not willing to pay taxes on their capital gains to the IRS. As a result, they rode the market all the way down and ended up gaining nothing, losing the opportunity of a lifetime because of their ideological beliefs.

The overall economy, which includes both stable (goods and services) and unstable (assets) sectors, lies somewhere between but leans strongly toward stability. The production and marketing of goods and services, the stable sectors, dominate our economy as measured by our Gross Domestic Product (GDP). Huge amounts of money are always changing hands in our financial markets, which include the futures markets for some commodities. Significant amounts also change hands in real estate markets. However, neither financial nor real estate markets dominate our overall economy and our GDP. Every once in a while, they can cause problems when speculation takes over, but most of the time they are not a source of difficulty. Hence, the overall economy tends to be stable.

But this raises the obvious question: Why do we have periods of recession and inflation? What causes periodic instability? Stay tuned; we'll answer this question later in this chapter.

#2—THE NARROW BAND

The aggregate economy fluctuates within a narrow band around its long-term trend—the growth rate of real Gross Domestic Product plus a minimal amount of inflation. Demand and supply shocks can cause the economy to move outside the narrow band. Once outside the band, however, it is very difficult to get back within the band, especially from above (when the economy has low unemployment and more than a minimal rate of inflation).

What should be our objective for the overall economy? What rate of growth for Gross Domestic Product (GDP) should we hope to achieve. There are two components here. The first is the long-term optimal growth rate for real GDP, which is about 2.5% per annum. The second is the desired maximum rate of inflation we are willing to accept. Let's say that it is 1% per annum, measured by an overall price index called the GNP deflator. Now we add together our real growth rate (2.5%) and acceptable rate of inflation (1%) to arrive at our goal of a 3.5% rate of growth for nominal GDP. Everyone would be happy if nominal GDP grew at a 3.5% annual rate in the long run so long as inflation was kept at 1% so that real growth would be at 2.5% per annum.

Now we have our goal—a long-term trend rate for nominal GDP of 3.5%. However, our economy tends to fluctuate a little around its long-term trend. Nothing can be done by government policy to prevent small fluctuations around this long-term trend. Frankly, economists do not know enough to completely stabilize a free market economy. (And as a conservative, I believe that we shouldn't interfere too much with free markets anyway.) My belief is that the economy, if left pretty much alone, will vary by no more than 1.5% from the long-term upward trend line of 3.5% per annum. That means that the economy will be expanding at somewhere between a 2% and 5% annual rate, averaging around 3.5% over time. This is the narrow band. Nominal GNP will fluctuate within the narrow band, not often hitting the band limits. All that is required is that we leave it alone and don't get hit by major demand or supply shocks. Leave the economy pretty much alone and it will usually stay within the narrow band.

Why? Why does the economy stay within the narrow band? Suppose the economy starts to drift downward from its optimal level of 3.5% growth in nominal GDP, 2.5% growth in real GDP and 1% inflation. Suppose real GDP is only rising at a 1.5% rate. The unemployment rate rises slightly, say from 6%, which we think of as full employment, toward 7%. Several little things happen to push the economy back in an upward direction:

- Unemployment compensation and welfare payments from the government increase a little.
- Employment tax collections fall a little.

The unemployment insurance program is an automatic stabilizer—a government program that automatically kicks in to push the economy in the direction opposite to which it is moving. When the economy is rising, the stabilizers pull downwards; when it is falling, as in our example, they push upwards.

- Interest rates fall a little and this causes business investment and consumer spending on durable goods to increase a little.
- Imports fall a little, leaving more spending for domestic goods.

The effects are all small, but they push the overall economy in an upward direction. They tend not only to prevent a little fluctuation from becoming a big fluctuation, but also to return economic activity back to its optimal growth rate.

What happens when the economy gets outside the narrow band? Suppose the economy suffers through a period of significant inflation (far more than the acceptable rate of 1% per annum) and we want to stop it. It is very difficult to use contractionary monetary and fiscal policies to ease our way gently back inside the narrow band. Public policy steps on the brakes and we drop right through the narrow band. We go into a period either of slow economic growth with real GDP growing at well under its optimal rate of 2.5% or even recession with real GDP actually falling. Now we face the problem of getting back into the narrow band from below. It is difficult to use expansionary monetary and fiscal policies to ease our way back inside the narrow band without overshooting and going right through it into inflation. Four things should be noted about getting back inside the narrow band:

- The farther we are away from the narrow band, the harder it is to get back inside without overshooting significantly.
- It is easier to get back into the narrow band from below than from above. It is easier to achieve stability without inflation after recession than to achieve stability without recession after inflation. In fact, America has never been able to stop a significant inflation without suffering a recession. Whenever we have achieved stability inside the narrow band, it has always been from below, coming out of a period of slow economic growth or recession. (The reason is that the rate of inflation, once established, is very resistant to reduction. Current wages and prices are often institutionally locked in and become a floor; they can rise much easier than they can fall.)
- Whenever we have recovered from recession and achieved stability within the narrow band, it has taken time to get there. Stabilizing the economy is a slow and gradual process. (Notice how long it is taking to recover from the Great Recession of 2008 with its high unemployment and slow economic growth.)
- We have a tendency for monetary and fiscal policies to regularly fluctuate between expansionary and contractionary stances. It is rarely "steady as she goes," which is what is needed to keep us within the narrow band.

There is an oddity to note here. Other nations struggle with their narrow bands, but their numbers can be quite different than ours. China is a less developed country with a very different kind of economy. It seeks real economic growth of about 9% per annum. It is willing to accept a bit more inflation than we do, say 4% per annum. And their narrow band seems to be wider than ours. So China's narrow band seems to be between an 11% and 15% growth rate of nominal GDP, a long way from our 2% to 5%.

Don't put great stock on the numbers used for China. They are my personal estimates and I am no expert on less developed countries and China. The differences between nations exist. The concept is important but the precise numbers are irrelevant.

#3—CAUSES OF INSTABILITY

Instability in the aggregate economy is caused by demand and supply shocks. Many of these come from foreign markets (exports and imports) and natural resource markets (for agricultural and mineral products, especially those related to energy). However, by far the most important shocks come from our own government's policies and changes in them.

A classic illustration of a supply shock was the combination earthquake and tsunami that rocked Japan and destroyed an important part of its nuclear power industry, causing real GDP to fall for quite some time. Clearly, Japan fell below its narrow band and took considerable time to get back into it. Another example of a supply shock is a crop failure induced by drought. Several countries have had this happen to them in 2012 with one of the worst hit being Australia, which struggled to maintain its real GDP and employment levels without falling into recession. Perhaps the most memorable American supply shock was the precipitous rise in oil prices in the mid-1970s, triggered by the political crisis and Arab-Israeli war in the Middle East. Few of us who lived through this period have forgotten the long lines at gas stations as our economy sputtered. It was then that Americans began to think in terms of smaller and more fuel-efficient automobiles and overall energy conservation.

There are few good examples of demand shocks that have been not only big enough to affect an economy as large and diverse as ours, but also were neither triggered nor caused by changes in public policy. We have had a couple of business investment booms and virtual explosions of automobile buying that have created overall prosperity and upward pressure on price levels, taking us above the narrow band. A demand shock affecting the entire world has been taking place for the last couple of years caused by the big increase in the demand for many natural resources triggered by the rapid expansion and development of the Chinese economy. This has been generating inflationary pressures around the world, enhanced by declining agricultural output in the face of drought in some of the key food-exporting nations, including the US.

While there are examples of demand and supply shocks that come from the private sector of the economy, the truth is that most of them are triggered and caused by public policy. To see why I can say that, let's sketch what has happened to the American economy over the past couple of decades. George H. W. Bush (the father) lost his presidency to Bill Clinton because he did nothing in the face of a minor recession and had raised taxes in spite of his pledge not to do so. The US economy eased into the narrow band from below and stayed there for the Clinton years—a very long period of prosperity historically. George W. Bush (the son) couldn't leave well enough alone. His administration lowered taxes and increased government spending, creating a large fiscal deficit that has haunted us to this day. The effects of this were compounded by the US undertaking two wars in the Middle East after 9/11. Our expansionary fiscal policy was enough to take us out of and above the narrow band. The Federal Reserve undertook an accommodating monetary policy to keep interest rates low, taking us farther above the narrow band. The Bush administration hated government regulation of the economy and thus both the financial and housing industries were effectively unregulated. The result was the perfect storm of four ingredients:

- highly expansionary fiscal policy;
- highly expansionary monetary policy;
- large financial institutions undertaking more and more risk in their asset portfolios; and
- the home-building industry building too many houses and selling them to unqualified borrowers financed by large mortgages.

The result was a very prosperous economy with booms in both the financial markets and home construction. Wonderful!

It all unraveled in 2007 and 2008. The housing market was the first casualty as many of the buyers who weren't really qualified for mortgages couldn't make their monthly payments. Home prices collapsed. Mortgages and securities based on them fell in value, some becoming virtually worthless. Large financial institutions holding these mortgages and mortgage-based securities suffered huge losses, some going bankrupt. The real economy started into freefall. Large manufacturing firms, especially the big three car companies, faced possible bankruptcy. We went into the Great Recession of 2008. Five years later, we still haven't recovered.

In a nutshell, what caused the Great Recession and the expansion that preceded it? What took us skyrocketing upwards out of the narrow band? Three things: bad fiscal policies; bad monetary policies; and bad regulation of our financial institutions and markets. Together, faulty government policies created an immense demand shock. When the speculative boom finally had run its course, the economy collapsed right through the narrow band into a deep recession. The federal government tried to right the ship with massive stimulation packages, bailouts of major financial institutions and two automobile companies, and expanded unemployment benefits. The Federal Reserve used quantitative easing, which is nothing more than a very expansionary monetary policy, to do its part. The results were both minimal and slow. It is difficult to get back into the narrow band, even from below (perhaps impossible from above) after a major economic disaster. Will we recover? Eventually, yes! However, it will take a very long time, but we have to hope that our government, including the Fed, doesn't screw up again along the way.

What is my personal conclusion about this? Just two things:
- A large and diverse economy like ours is subject to a certain minimal amount of instability caused by demand and supply shocks, but is inherently stable in that most fluctuations are relatively small and short-lived.
- It is faulty government polices that cause demand and supply shocks of a magnitude large enough to generate truly major fluctuations in

the level of economic activity—things like the Great Depression of the 1930s and our recent Great Recession.

What is the solution for economic instability? For small economic fluctuations, there is none; we have to accept a little instability. For large fluctuations, the solution is to keep the government from screwing up its economic policies. And that includes the Fed.

Our description of the causes of the Great Recession is a short and simplified one. There are several good books dealing with what happened in detail. My favorite was the paperback edition of "Freefall", containing added materials on the aftermath, written by Joseph Stiglitz, a winner of the Nobel Prize in Economics. He blames our large financial institutions every bit as much as our inadequate public policies for what happened in the last decade.

In my opinion, faulty monetary and fiscal policies are the primary causes of instability in the economies of developed countries, especially the larger ones. However, a wide range of public policies can be the culprits in a given situation. We have already mentioned how our regulatory policies, or lack thereof, were a major factor causing the Great Recession. Much of Europe's instability is caused by its rigid labor market policies and welfare-state mentality. Other policies having destabilizing effects can be those relating to world trade, agriculture, energy and environmentalism. Of course, the larger, the more diverse, and the more advanced the economy, the more likely that flawed fiscal and monetary policies are the key to economic instability.

#4—THE UPPER-LIMIT

Politics in a democracy causes policymakers to support policies that push the economy towards the upper limit of the narrow band in the short run in order to raise the levels of real GDP and employment (lowering the rate of unemployment). The result is that the narrow band moves upward and the rate of inflation increases but real GDP remains unaffected, at least in the long run. Thus, democracies always have an inflationary bias to their economic policies.

Even if our political leaders understood the concept of the narrow band and the need to allow the economy to fluctuate a little around its long-term trend (and they don't), they would always support policies that push us toward the upper limit of the narrow band. If we were operating optimally at 3.5% growth of nominal GDP with 2.5% real growth, 1% inflation and 6% unemployment, most politicians in the administration and Congress would want nominal GDP to grow at 5% per annum in the hope that real growth could be increased to 3% and unemployment reduced to 5%. They wouldn't worry that inflation might rise to 2% or more. Not only will they support fiscal policies that work toward this objective, they will also pressure the Fed to ease monetary policy for that purpose. Oddly enough, doing this can work so that growth rates rise and unemployment rates fall.......but only for a short while. Then real output returns to its long-term optimal growth rate of 2.5% and the unemployment rate goes back to 6%. However, we are left with a higher inflation rate of about 2.5%. In effect, the narrow band rises to accommodate the higher rate of nominal GDP growth. This process can continue so long as society is willing to accept rising rates of inflation, but eventually everyone has had enough. Then contractionary policies are initiated to cure inflation and we drop through the narrow band into recession with lower real output and higher unemployment. This has happened all too often in history, both here and abroad.

After leading the United States and free world into a successful war to free Kuwait from Saddam Hussein, George H. W. Bush (the father) reached unprecedented levels of popularity in the polls, but was denied reelection by Bill Clinton because of two things. First, he promised to not raise taxes ("Read my lips.") but did. Second, he didn't do anything to combat a minor recession in the belief that the economy would get back to its optimal growth rate on its own. The general public expects its leaders to be concerned and take action whenever any little thing goes wrong. President Bush understood the economics of the upper-limit postulate but seemingly did not grasp the politics of the public desire for action in the face of any adversity. Subsequent presidents have realized that people in general want their political leaders to take action whenever anything goes wrong. And that is why democracies have an inflationary bias.

#5—TIME LAGS

Because of long and variable time lags, fiscal and monetary policies cannot be used effectively to stabilize the economy in the short

run. Government policies of all kinds affect the economy (the level of economic activity) but the effects are generally slow to take effect. The analogy is that of the movement of a very large ship. Its momentum makes it continue on its same course at its same speed. It takes a long time to either accelerate or slow down. The economy also has momentum and it takes a long time to either expand or contract.

Whenever stabilization policy is to be used, there is a problem of long time lags. In essence, there are at least five major time lags between need and full impact:

- The recognition lag is the time between when a problem emerges and when policy makers realize that there is a problem.
- The decision lag is the time between when policy makers realize that they have a problem and when they decide what to do about it.
- The implementation lag is the time between a policy decision and its execution.
- The initial impact lag is the time between when a policy action is implemented and when noticeable effects occur.
- The maximum impact lag is the time between beginning to see some impact and policy having its full effect.

The first three lags—recognition, decision and implementation— are usually grouped together and collectively called the inside lag. They take place inside the decision-making agencies. The last two lags—initial impact and maximum impact—are grouped together and thought of as the outside lag. They take place outside the decision-making agencies and in the overall economy.

Monetary policy is generally thought to have a relatively short inside lag. Policy decisions are made by economists and bankers who are members of the Open Market Committee of the Federal Reserve Board. They have good forecasting models and economic data at their fingertips; hence, the recognition lag is usually short. They meet regularly to discuss policy; hence, the decision lag is usually short. It takes only a few days after a decision is made to initiate a change in policy; hence, the implementation lag is also usually short. The inside lag for monetary policy is thus quite short. The outside lag is quite another matter. Initial impact probably takes somewhere up to a year, while maximum impact will not occur for up to about three years. The overall result is that monetary policy moves the economy slowly and thus can only be used for major economic disturbances, not for "fine tuning" the economy in the short run.

For fiscal policy, the time lag problem is quite different. Here, politicians—both in the administration and Congress—are at the helm of the decision-making apparatus. They are usually slow in recognizing even the most significant of economic problems. Once they recognize that there is a problem, then decision-making is near impossible because:

- Liberal politicians want to increase government spending and taxes while conservative politicians want to reduce government spending and taxes.
- All politicians fight to get benefits for their constituents and the special interests that provide financial and political support.

Implementation can be a problem, but is usually shorter for changes in taxes and transfer payments than for changes in expenditures. Anyway, the inside lag for fiscal policy is usually extremely long. The outside lag is usually somewhat shorter for fiscal than for monetary policy, with both the initial and maximum impact lags being comparatively shorter. However, because of time lags, fiscal policy also can only be used for major economic disturbances, not for "fine tuning" the economy in the short run.

#6—POLICY EFFECTIVENESS

Fiscal and monetary policies are relatively ineffective as instruments for affecting the level of national income (GDP) and stabilizing the economy in the short run. The effects of fiscal policy are fairly immediate but relatively small. The effects of monetary policy are somewhat stronger, especially for contractionary purposes, but are relatively delayed. Fiscal and monetary policies are more effective when they are coordinated than when they are used independent of each other.

This postulate involves more economic analysis than any of the others. So we are going to break it down and simplify the material. Each of the following paragraphs will start by asking a simple question to be answered in the following material; that should keep everything pretty easy.

What does stabilization policy do? The federal government uses fiscal and monetary policies to stabilize our economy. Expansionary policies are used to make national income (GDP—Gross Domestic Product) rise and unemployment rates fall, but tend to cause the rate of inflation to increase. Contractionary policies are used to make the rate of inflation fall, but tend to cause national income to fall and the unemployment rate to rise. Notice that there are always perverse effects of stabilization policy.

What are expansionary policies? An expansionary monetary policy involves an increase in the money supply (or its rate of growth) and a reduction in interest rates. An expansionary fiscal policy has three dimensions:
- increased government expenditures;
- reduced taxes on consumers and increased transfer payments to consumers (reduced net taxes on households); and
- reduced taxes on businesses and increased subsidies to businesses (reduced net taxes on businesses).

What are contractionary policies? Contractionary stabilization policies would involve reductions in the money supply (or its rate of growth), increased interest rates, reduced government expenditures, increased net taxes on households, and increased net taxes on businesses.

What is the effect of an expansionary fiscal policy? An expansionary fiscal policy causes national income (GDP) to rise, but the effects are smaller than most people believe. An increase in government spending of $100B causes national income (GDP) to increase by that $100B. There are secondary effects but they tend to offset each other, although they may cause a small additional increase in GDP before falling back, creating a wave-like movement in GDP over time. A reduction in household and business taxes of $100B causes national income (GDP) to increase by less than $100B. The effect is probably in the range of $60B to $80B. As in the case of an increase in government spending, the secondary effects essentially offset each other but may create a small wave-like movement in national income. The net effects of an expansionary fiscal policy are that national income increases approximately dollar-for-dollar in the case of higher government spending and less than dollar-for-dollar with reduced taxes. We should note that expansionary fiscal policy puts upward pressure on interest rates. (The effects of a contractionary fiscal policy are the precise opposite of those for expansionary policy.)

> Just because we are using numbers to illustrate the effects, do not put much faith in the accuracy of these numbers. They reflect a consensus view among economists, but the range of possible effects in a particular situation is huge.

What is the effect of monetary policy? If you believe that our analysis of the effects of fiscal policy is nebulous at best, wait until you hear what we have to say about monetary policy. It is very difficult to use numbers to illustrate the effects of monetary policy. If we increase the rate of growth of the money supply by about 2% per annum, eventually after a long and highly variable time lag, we would expect national income to be also rising faster by about 2% per annum. We can only conclude that:

1. The effects of monetary policy are somewhat stronger than those for fiscal policy in the case of contractionary policies.
2. The effects of monetary policy are somewhat weaker than those for fiscal policy in the case of expansionary policies.
3. The effects of monetary policy are back loaded, building slowly over time, taking between one and three years before the full effects are felt, especially for expansionary policies.
4. An expansionary monetary policy causes interest rates to fall at first but they tend to come back up after a lag. Likewise, a contractionary policy causes interest rates to rise but eventually to fall back, at least partially.

Note the difference between contractionary and expansionary monetary policies. The former is stronger and much more definite than the latter. Economists use the analogy of pulling on a string rather than pushing with a string. They also say that you can lead a horse to water but cannot make it drink. Making money and credit available to households and businesses does not necessarily mean that they will increase their spending.

What happens if monetary and fiscal policies work together? So far, we have analyzed fiscal and monetary policies separately, examining what happens when we change the one without any change in the other. What happens when they work together? This is most likely to occur in periods of recession or slow economic growth, when policy makers all look toward expansionary actions. So let's look at this case. Expansionary fiscal policy causes national income to increase, albeit modestly but as desired. It also causes interest rates to rise. This increase in interest rates triggers secondary effects that reduce the desired increase in national income significantly. If the Fed also has an expansionary monetary policy, the effect will be to cause national income to increase, again modestly but as desired, but it also causes interest rates to fall, especially in the short run. Putting the policies together, expansionary fiscal policy causes interest rates to increase while expansionary monetary policy causes rates to fall. The two effects cancel each other out and thus interest rates stay relatively constant and the weakening secondary effects are eliminated. Hence, the impact is a much stronger increase in income. When the Fed acts in concert with an expansionary fiscal policy, it is called "monetizing the deficit." In effect, the Fed is printing money for the Treasury to finance the resulting fiscal deficit.

#7—THE SUPPLY SIDE

Fiscal and monetary policies have their primary impacts upon aggregate demand, but all economic policies influence aggregate supply, primarily because they affect our stock of physical and human capital as well as behavioral incentives.

Fiscal policy especially has major supply-side effects. What we spend money on matters. Government spending on infrastructure (transportation, communication and public utility facilities), human capital (education, training and health), and research and development (especially basic research) have significant positive effects on aggregate supply in the long run. What we tax also matters. If we taxed consumption rather than personal income, we would have a greater incentive to save more and consume less. Since saving ultimately becomes investment, capital accumulation increases and real GDP rises in the long run. If we increase transfer payments like welfare and disability benefits, people getting funds from these programs have less incentive to work. The supply of labor is reduced and our potential real output is also lowered. Minimum wage laws affect the supply of labor, especially teenagers and those with disabilities. Environmental laws have large impacts on business costs and thus what can and will be produced. Subsidies to business increase the production of goods that typically cannot make it in a free market (ethanol is a prime example). Virtually all economic policies, whether laws or regulations, affect aggregate supply in the long run.

Conservative Republicans talk a lot about supply-side economics, but it was a liberal Democrat who made first use of it in this country. Faced with a stagnating economy that had given us three recessions in eight years, President John Kennedy initiated investment tax credits and accelerated depreciation allowances to successfully increase business investment, capital accumulation and the rate of economic growth. Subsequently, President Ronald Reagan used deregulation successfully to lower business costs and promote economic growth. Both of these presidents initiated solid periods of economic prosperity by following supply-side policies.

#8—CAUSE OF INFLATION

Inflation is a general and continuing reduction in the value of money. It can be triggered by demand and supply shocks in domestic and world markets—not only by increases in aggregate demand caused by expansionary fiscal policies and bursts of market demand for our exports, capital goods, and consumer durables, including housing; but also by reductions in aggregate supply caused by energy shortages, crop failures, business monopoly power and natural disasters. No matter how it is triggered, however, for inflation to be sustained, it must always be accompanied and caused by increases in the supply of money. In advanced economies, all prolonged and major inflations are caused by expansionary monetary policies. In this sense, inflation is always a monetary phenomenon.

What happens if we experience a major shock that triggers inflation but the monetary authorities (the Fed) do not expand the money supply? Let's examine the plausible case of a major rise in energy prices, say a doubling of the price of oil caused by war in the Middle East. Virtually all businesses, especially those with high transportation expenses, find that their costs have risen precipitously and immediately. They raise their prices to cover their higher costs. The price level rises to cover the higher costs of energy. At the same time, virtually all consumers find their outlays at the gas station (and for heating oil at home in the winter) rising. They cut back on expenditures on other things, especially durable goods. Their real incomes have fallen. Thus, the economy as a whole suffers a burst of rising prices and falling real income. But if the Fed does not expand the money supply, this is the end of the story. We move to a higher price level but there is no continuing or sustained inflation. That takes an increase in the rate of growth of the money supply.

If the Fed expands the money supply at the same rate that real GDP is growing in the long run, about 2.5% per annum, the price level will stay pretty much constant over time and we will not suffer from sustained inflation. If the Fed increases the rate of growth of the money supply to 6% per annum, we will tend to have an inflation of about 3.5% per annum—the rate of growth of the money supply minus the rate of growth of real GDP. (There is a strong relationship between monetary growth rates and the rate of inflation, but it is not a perfect relationship. Hence, our numerical examples are indicative but not exact.)

If expanding the money supply faster tends to cause inflation, why then does the Fed expand the money supply faster? It does so in an attempt to increase real GDP and lower interest rates in the short run. The Fed is always under pressure from politicians, the financial markets and even the general public to undertake expansionary policies. But any positive effects are fleeting. Real GDP will not grow more than about 2.5% per annum in the long run. Interest rates will inevitably rise again.

Thus it is that a significant and sustained inflation can always be blamed on excessively expansionary monetary policy and the monetary authorities. In the US, the Fed is the source of inflation.

#9—LONG-TERM POLICY ORIENTATION

Public policy would be vastly improved if it had a long-term rather than a short-term orientation. Unfortunately, politicians only see as far as the next election and thus support actions with their major benefits in the short run and their main costs in the long run. One of the important short-run benefits of any political move is the public perception that the government is doing something about a problem, no matter whether or not it is helping or hurting society, particularly in the long run. (What this means in many cases is that political benefits occur in the short run but economic costs take place in the long run.) Let's examine three examples of the long-term postulate currently at work in America:

- The Patient Protection and Affordable Care Act (Obamacare) was not only politically popular with liberals but also made some immediate positive changes in medical care (policies re existing conditions and young people). However, its major costs were all postponed until after the 2012 election. The most important problem it created for the long run was that it significantly increased the demand for medical treatment without doing anything to increase the supply, making some form of rationing inevitable since normal pricing mechanisms do not function in the medical fields.

- Politicians everywhere have supported pension plans with defined benefits rather than defined contributions. This kept the cost of pensions down in the short run when there were few retired people, but has come back to haunt the public sector as more and more of us are retiring. This is the essence of the difficulties we are having with Social Security at the federal level and with municipal bankruptcies at the lower level (not to mention a few states, such as California, with horrendous financial problems).

- Our immigration policies are ridiculous, and we are not talking about illegal but legal immigration. America gives priority in immigration to refugees and the extended families of those already in this country. Many of these immigrants are poorly educated and will be a burden to our society. We make highly-educated and valuable employees of major corporations (that want to bring key people from abroad to headquarters in this country) wait for years to obtain legal entry into the US. The same applies to entrepreneurial types who want to start high-end businesses in this country. Compare our policies with those of Canada and Chile (Yes, Chile!) that go out of their way to bring the best and the brightest into the fold.

#10—ADJUSTMENT COSTS

No matter how beneficial, most changes in policy impose significant costs of adjustment on someone. This provides a good reason for phasing in changes in policy over time rather than all at once.

Giving people and businesses time to respond helps them to come into conformity with the new public policies. Let's look at three examples to get the point across:

Tariff Reduction. The US imposes tariffs on sugar. As a result, Americans pay more for sugar than they should and there is a profitable domestic sugar industry with a significant number of employees. In the interests of free trade, we should eliminate most tariffs, including the one on sugar. The result would be as follows:

- consumers would be better off because the price of sugar would fall,
- lower-cost foreign suppliers would displace domestic producers,
- people in the sugar industry would lose their jobs and investment.

The third effect is the adjustment cost. We would be better off by spreading the reduction in sugar tariffs over time (say 10% every six months) than by eliminating the tariff all at once. We get the long-term benefits but minimize the short-term costs.

Fixing Social Security. We all know that we need to do something to change Social Security as the number of recipients increases over time and the number of workers paying in declines. Because people are living longer, we need to increase the retirement age. But raising it from 65 to 70 in one fell swoop is grossly unfair to those who are close to retirement age. Therefore, the way to do it is to spread it out. For those over 60, the retirement age could be raised 6 months; for over 55, a year; for over 50, 18 months; for over 45, 2 full years; etc. This would enable people to adjust their retirement plans while going a long way to fixing Social Security.

Water Shortages. Much of the American West suffers from inadequate water supplies. The problem is a simple one: there are too many people using too much water in an arid region. Water has always been treated by people as a free good and thus it is overused. Too many people in Southern California and Arizona hose down their driveways to keep them clean. Too many farmers have water-intensive crops (like growing rice in California's Central Valley). Too much water has been allocated to the Indians by treaty. We as a society need to pay more for water to solve the long-term water problem. But to double the price of a basic necessity would definitely hurt low-income people. So we need to raise the price of water, not just to households but also to agriculture and business, and do so in automatic steps over a considerable period of time. This will keep the hurt down and allow people in agriculture and business to adjust their budgets and product pricing gradually.

#11—INCENTIVES VERSUS RULES

When government wants to change business or human behavior, it is more effective to use economic incentives than to impose rules and regulations for three reasons:

1. With incentives, people and businesses will almost always change in the desired direction.
2. With rules and regulations, people and businesses will not only favor minimum compliance over steady improvement but also use legal means as a tactic for delaying and opposing the enforcement of government policy.
3. Rules and regulations require a larger government bureaucracy than incentives programs.

Unfortunately, both political parties prefer rules and regulations over financial incentives, liberal Democrats because they believe in big government and are heavily supported by the legal profession, conservative Republicans because they see most financial incentives as taxation programs. As a result, when seeking to control business and human behavior, American government always seems to choose methods that are less effective, more bureaucratic, and thus more expensive. Let's again use examples to prove our point:

Gas Mileages. We want our vehicles to burn less gasoline because of pollution and the high cost of imports. We use control of fleet averages for miles per gallon (MPG), a bureaucratic rule to force the car companies to comply. However, wouldn't it be easier if we sought a 30 mpg average to tax and subsidize car prices depending on the vehicle's MPG. A car getting 25 MPG would pay a tax of $500—$100 per MPG below the target. One getting 35 MPG would get a subsidy of $500—$100 per MPG above the target. Notice three things about such a program:

• Car prices would reflect society's desire for using less oil; consumers would gradually shift their preferences in the socially-desirable direction.

- The target MPG could gradually be increased over time as needed.
- The program could be made revenue neutral and so would not increase government tax revenue.

Air Pollution. If we really want to reduce the amount of air pollution created by electric power plants, why not just impose a tax of every ton of particulate and other harmful emissions? We have the technology to measure such emissions. Just tax them! The power companies would have an incentive to reduce their emissions, not just up to the regulated maximum but well beyond. We could readily institute the tax system gradually to minimize the shock and cost of adjustment, which ultimately must be borne by consumers in their electric bills.

It is truly deplorable that the general public and our elected officials understand so little about economics. Many of our socially-desirable programs could be improved—made more effective and reduced in cost—by applying some simple principles of economic analysis to them.

#12—INSTABILITY PROMOTES GROWTH

In a free market economy, some short-term economic instability facilitates long-term economic growth. Over time, the economy fluctuates even while staying within the narrow band. Small downturns (with falling employment and business profits) are followed by small upticks (with rising employment and business profits) Small economic downturns, staying within the narrow band, help weed out obsolete and unprofitable businesses, some contracting and some failing completely, freeing resources (both labor and capital) for new and expanding enterprises. In the following upturn, entrepreneurs and managers in the business sector become optimistic. As a result, new businesses are formed and existing firms expand, taking advantage of the resources that have become available. As a general rule, these new businesses are more productive than those older businesses that contracted or ceased operations. Hence, the rate of economic growth tends to increase and society as a whole is better off. Joseph Schumpeter, one of history's more notable economists, called this the process of creative destruction and considered it to be a major factor in the processes of economic growth.

Of course, major business cycles that take us well outside the narrow band have far larger economic downturns that cause not only far more worker unemployment but also significant numbers of business contractions and failures. Larger quantities of labor and capital resources are freed up and made available for the following period of prosperity. Creative destruction takes place on a larger scale and this does enhance economic growth in the long run. Nevertheless, the short-run costs of increased unemployment and failing firms are so significant that they almost certainly exceed the benefits of enhanced economic growth in the long run. We can conclude simply that a little bit of economic instability (staying inside the narrow band) is socially beneficial and desirable, but that major business fluctuations (taking us out of the narrow band) are not.

11

PROGRAM FOR AMERICA

This is a very personalized chapter. Its primary subject matter is what just one person believes needs to be done with public policy to make the United States of America into a better society. Its orientation is on the conservative side, although some of what is being proposed leans toward being liberal. The analysis is not that deep, but what is proposed is supported by brief statements as to why such is needed and socially desirable, at least in the author's opinion. The material is divided into four sections:

- Constitutional amendments;
- reform of the three big domestic programs—Social Security, Medicare and Medicaid;
- some socially-desirable changes in priorities; and
- the role of government in stabilization and regulation.

This is where the author gets on a soap box and uses what he has been writing about for ten chapters to discuss some possible policy implications and changes.

Two short segments have been added to this chapter. The first is a detailing of eight major problems with economic, social and political implications that concern me but are beyond the purview of this book. The chapter and book end with a simple summary of the dozen lessons that the author would like to have his readers come away with from their reading of his writings, followed by a grand bottom-line conclusion.

CONSTITUTIONAL AMENDMENTS

There are four constitutional amendments that the author believes this country should undertake:

LINE ITEM VETO. This amendment would allow the President to veto or reduce (but not increase) any specific expenditure item in the budget presented to him by the Congress. Currently, the President can either accept and sign the budget or veto it completely, requiring Congress to start over. The advantage of having a line item veto is simply that someone would have to accept responsibility for the amount of federal government spending and the social waste of many earmarked expenditures such as the famous "bridge to nowhere." It is sad that we have to resort to measures such as this to limit government spending, but our politicians in both parties have failed to demonstrate any form of restraint. With the line item veto, we will be able to point a finger and say it is your responsibility to someone in authority, namely the President.

OPEN PRIMARIES. Washington is full of extremists. Most of the Democrats there are extreme liberals; most of the Republicans are extreme conservatives. Moderates are few and far between. That is because the extremists in both parties dominate the primary process. Extremists win both primaries and then face off, leaving moderates in both parties and independents with little choice but to hold their nose and choose the best horse in the glue factory. Having open primaries would bring moderates in both parties and independents into the fray. The two top vote getters would then face off. In strongly liberal districts, we might end up with two Democrats facing each other in the November election; in conservative districts it might be two Republicans. In either case, however, at least one of them is almost certain to be a moderate. Since more moderates who are likely to be willing to compromise with each other would be elected, open primaries should end most of the gridlock in Washington. We might even be able to get our politicians to do something worthwhile for a change.

TERM LIMITS. Too many of our representatives in Washington are professional politicians. All they have ever done is politics. They have little real world experience in business, education, unionism, agriculture, or the practice of law. Or even as a housewife. We would benefit by having more diversity in Congress. We would benefit from having those who write our various rules and regulations, including our tax code, have to live with them like the rest of us. Someone who is a business person or lawyer could spend a few years in Washington and then return to his or her business or law practice. All it would take is term limits—say four two-year terms in the House of Representatives and two six-year terms in the Senate. We already limit the President to two four-year terms, so why not limit all our politicians? Many of us would rather have rank amateurs representing us than the kind of professionalism we now have.

ELECTORAL COLLEGE REFORM. We know well in advance for which party many of the states will vote in our presidential elections. These red and blue states are so predictable that they see little campaigning by the candidates for President and Vice President. It is ridiculous to have the major candidates avoiding our largest states—California, New York, Texas—just because they almost always vote the same way. All the candidates' time is spent seeking votes in the five to ten swing states which will decide any close election. This happens because all a state's electoral votes go to the winners of the state. What is proposed to correct this is to have one electoral vote for each congressional district and two electoral votes for the overall winner of each state. This would require our major party nominees to campaign all across the nation and not take anything for granted. It would mean that voting becomes more meaningful for many of us who happen to live in states that are predictable in their voting patterns.

There is one constitutional amendment that has been talked about, especially among conservatives, that should definitely not be adopted. That is the Balanced Budget Amendment. It would require that the federal government balance its annual budget, not running a deficit and not increasing the national debt. It is easy to understand the frustration of conservatives with the proclivity of politicians to spend too much (especially liberal politicians) and tax too little (especially conservative politicians). Nevertheless, none of us with an understanding of economics can accept such a proposal because it would destroy the effectiveness and utilization of fiscal policy. If the economy were to go into a recession, even a minor one that stays within the narrow band, tax revenue would fall and transfer payments would rise, creating a fiscal deficit. This is what the automatic stabilizers do to keep the economy within the narrow band. At such a time of recession, to require the federal government to either reduce expenditures, including transfer payments, or increase taxes is anything but beneficial. It would be procyclical, making the recession worse, rather than countercyclical, reducing the size of the recession. Doing such a thing would be plain stupid, if not political suicide.

The four constitutional amendments proposed here may be the right thing for the long-run future of America and, once explained in detail, may become acceptable to and even popular with the general public. However, the amendments will never be popular with our professional politicians because the political power of the parties and incumbents is being restricted. Change in our legal and institutional structure will never get the support of those whose jobs depend on it. Changing the Constitution without the backing of politicians is extremely difficult, as it should be. So what is needed to get the job done—to get the Constitution changed? Two things: leadership and money! Lots of money! Lots and lots of money! So where might the leadership and money come from? There is only one possible source that I can see. This country has a large number of billionaires. Many of them know and are friendly with each other. Many of them have established charitable foundations to support various causes here and around the world. If a group of them agreed that there is a need to change things in this country, if that group was willing to provide significant chunks of money to a good domestic cause, and if that group was willing to work together, something remarkable just might happen. Let's face it, many Americans are unhappy with the direction American politics is going and would support a movement to seek productive change. There is a relatively short list of very wealthy Americans who could lead the charge. It will take a group of these people stepping up to provide the two things needed—leadership and money. But the potential for the future is boundless.

REFORM OF THE "BIG THREE"

After national defense, the three biggest spending programs of the federal government are Social Security, Medicare and Medicaid. As our population ages and as medical costs inflate, we need to reform all three, primarily to make them viable in the long run but also to provide some budget relief in the short run. Let's look at all three programs briefly, concentrating on alternative approaches to reform.

SOCIAL SECURITY. Our national retirement system has a major problem in the long run, namely that the number of people paying into the retirement fund is falling relative to the number receiving benefits. There once was a day when we had thirty people paying taxes by payroll deduction for every one receiving a pension. That number has fallen considerably and will someday reach two paying in for each of us being paid to. That is not financially feasible. The alternative changes in Social Security to fix its financial problems include four choices:

1. raising more revenue by either increasing the payroll tax or taxing investment income as well as wage income (say by taxing income from interest payments and dividends over some minimum and below some maximum—perhaps from $100,000 to $1 million);
2. reducing benefits—the size of pensions;
3. imposing means testing so that those who are well off would not receive benefits even though they had paid into the system all their lives—changing Social Security from an insurance plan to a welfare system; and
4. raising the retirement age so that people would pay in longer and receive benefits for a shorter time—doing so gradually so that people's retirement plans would not be too disrupted—say by raising the retirement age by one year for those in their sixties, by two years for those in their fifties, by three years for those in their forties, etc.

Since people are living longer, raising the retirement age seems to be a certainty, but that can be combined with one of the other three alternatives.

MEDICARE. Our national health insurance for seniors is very expensive, costing about $11,000 per enrollee and a total of over $500 billion per annum, with about a quarter of all outlays going for end-of-life care. There are at least four alternative approaches to reform of Medicare:

1. vouchers—giving every old person a voucher for a set amount of money to pay for private medical insurance;
2. reduced payments to health providers—doctors, hospitals, care facilities, etc.;
3. higher ages for coverage--like those suggested for Social Security; and
4. more out-of-pocket payments for medical treatment—patients would pay some percentage of all treatment costs up to some maximum (10% up to $1,500) or the first (perhaps) $100 of each month's treatment costs.

As an economist, I have to like the last alternative because medical care would no longer be a free good that is overused by old people. If we had to pay part of the cost, we would think twice about going to the doctor for every little ache and pain.

MEDICAID. Our national health program for the indigent and low-income families is funded jointly by the federal and state governments, but is administered by the states under federal rules. It is needs-based and means-tested. It is expensive but not that controversial. However, many of the states would be quite willing to accept less funding from the federal government if they didn't have to live with so many stringent federal rules. This would allow each state to tailor its program to its own circumstances and to experiment to find better ways of providing medical care for those who are less well off. Allowing greater flexibility is the major approach under consideration for reforming Medicaid.

Without getting into the political debate about Obamacare—the Patient Protection and Affordable Care Act—I would be remiss as an economist if I didn't point out one salient fact. Obamacare will increase the demand for medical treatment but does nothing to increase the supply. The economic result is inevitable. Either the price of medical care will increase or, if price controls are used to keep medical prices down, there will be shortages of medical care. Treatment will be rationed in one way or another. There are three possibilities and all of them would be very unpopular:

1. treatment will be given to those who are best able to pay;
2. treatment will be given only after very long waits (and some of the patients waiting will die off); or
3. who gets treatment will be determined by some public agency (which will literally have the power to decide life or death).

Pick your poison!

CHANGING PRIORITIES

In my view, we need to change our priorities in at least five significant areas. The first two involve reductions in government expenditures that could be used to pay for the two following expansions of public spending. The final item relates to the need to raise more tax revenue for the federal government.

NATIONAL DEFENSE. The United States spends three times more on national defense than the four most likely irritants we might ever have to face—China, Russia, Iran and North Korea—combined. And that doesn't even count our spending on wars in Iraq and Afghanistan. In fact, we account for just under half of all defense and military expenditures worldwide. While doing this may help keep us safe (and that point is debated by some), we pay a high opportunity cost in terms of what we have to give up in our domestic expenditures, and a lower rate of economic growth—a reduced Gross Domestic Product in the long run. We should do six things to reduce our spending on national defense, with the last being the most important:

- Reduce the number of military bases both overseas and at home. (Being an avid golfer, I won't get into privatizing some of the over 200 golf courses run by the military.)
- Reduce the number of naval battle fleets based around our large aircraft carriers from ten to eight. We have used the naval fleet (previously known as the great white fleet) to demonstrate our strength around the world for a century, but it's time to limit ourselves.
- Reduce the number of attack and ballistic missile submarines in service. Let's decommission them one per quarter for two to three years. We will still have the largest and best silent service in the world.
- Retire half the generals and admirals serving in Washington. They are little more than very expensive bureaucrats pushing paper around and around.
- Eliminate our Veterans Hospitals. We should privatize the best of them and close the rest, relying on the vast nonmilitary network of hospitals to provide improved medical care for our military personnel, veterans, and their families.
- Be less willing to be the world's policeman. It's a thankless task and we are hated for doing it anyway. If something needs to be done, let's work through the United Nations, NATO, or some other alliance. It worked well in Libya when Britain and France took the lead and we provided support behind the scene. Our influence on what happens is relatively small in many cases, so let's recognize that fact and mind our own business. We are not the world's conscience.

All of this cannot be done at once, perhaps not in a single presidential term. Change takes time. We should do it gradually to minimize adjustment costs. But let's get it done!

BUYING MILITARY HARDWARE

Modern weapons systems are almost incomprehensively expensive. Just look at the figures for four of the key pieces of military equipment currently planned by the Pentagon and already in production:

- The F-35 stealth jet fighter has an average cost of over $160 million each. Plans are to build over 2,400 of them at a total cost of just under $400 billion. The program is expected to cost over $1.5 trillion during the life of the program.
- Aircraft carriers cost $14 billion each. That doesn't include the cost of the aircraft they will carry or the ships that make up the support fleet for each of them. Three are on order at a total cost of $42 billion.
- Attack submarines cost over $3 billion each. The Navy has ordered 30 of them at a total cost of $93 billion.
- The V-22 tilt-rotor helicopter costs $115 million each. The armed forces are buying over 450 at a total cost of $53 billion.[1]

While the numbers are interesting, they don't tell the full story. The cost of each of the above high-tech programs will steadily rise over time. That is what always happens when the government buys military equipment. The specifications change and the costs rise as new features are added to the hardware.

As an illustration of what takes place, let's look at five major problems with the F-35 program, the single most expensive weapons system in the history of the world:

- The F-35 is a single airplane trying to meet three very distinct needs. The Air Force wants a fighter and medium bomber with long-range capabilities. The Navy wants a reconnaissance fighter that is sturdy enough to land on aircraft carriers. The Marines want a fighter that can replace the Harrier, which can land and take off vertically from small areas. These needs are incompatible with each other. So the F-35 becomes a jack of all trades but master of none. Each of the three planned versions of the plane is compromised.

- The F-35 is designed for stealth, which is an outmoded technology. Detection methods are improving so quickly that there will be no such thing as being able to hide from the enemy in future conflicts.
- The F-35 is designed for the last war—the global Cold War against the military might of Soviet Russia. It will be virtually useless for dealing with localized smaller conflicts and terrorists. Drones will be the future weapon of choice because they are less expensive and expendable since they don't make use of a pilot.
- Technology is changing so quickly that the F-35 is being built while it is still being designed. There is no final set of blueprints for the planes that are on the production line. And there are over 24 million lines of computer code involved in those blueprints. Obviously, nothing could go wrong there!
- Making the F-35 program financially viable requires that many of our allies buy and make use of the airplane. Because of the high price tag, however, Canada and Australia are already backing away from their acquisition plans and increasingly willing to go with existing F-15, F-16 and F-18 technology.

Given all of these problems, is there any chance that Congress will terminate the program? Of course not! After all, the F-35 is being built in 45 of the 50 states and no politician is going to vote to end a program that generates jobs in his or her jurisdiction.

PRISONS. At over 2.3 million, the United States has the largest prison population in the world. That means that one of every 100 adults in America is incarcerated. Just look at the numbers for the three most populous nations in the world:

	Population	Prisoners
China	1.35 billion	about 1.5 million
India	1.25 billion	less than 400,000
USA	315 million	above 2.3 million

We won't even get into the high proportion of young black and Hispanic males in confinement. We spend $75 billion annually on jails, prisons, and correctional facilities. Yet, our prisons are overcrowded; California has over 150,000 inmates in facilities designed for less than 90,000 prisoners. There seems to be four primary reasons why America has so many prison inmates:

- Our politicians in both parties like to appear tough on crime.
- We have "the right to bear arms" and own guns, including high-powered weapons that have no possible use other than killing people.
- We imprison people for using recreational drugs, not just for manufacturing and selling illegal drugs.
- Our white population is afraid of ethnic minorities.
- We consider ourselves to be "the land of the free." Oh, really?

INFRASTRUCTURE. This country needs to spend more on its infrastructure. Our electrical transmission grid is antiquated. Our bridges are in disrepair. Our rail system is stretched to its capacity for freight but is underutilized for passenger service. We have too much water and floods in some places; too little water and either droughts or shortages in others. Increased spending in these areas increases the rate of economic growth in the long run. And it doesn't matter that much whether the spending is private, public, or induced by government tax and subsidy incentives.

RESEARCH AND DEVELOPMENT. As a society, we need to spend more on research and development. R&D has three distinct parts:

1. Invention. This involves the expansion of scientific knowledge and arises from basic research. It is a product of individual brilliance (the name Steven Jobs comes to mind), large corporate and public research laboratories, and research grants financed by government and various private sources.

2. Innovation. This involves applying new knowledge to original practical uses. It is usually done by business and is especially prevalent among start-up firms financed by investors seeking to hit it big.

3. Diffusion. This involves spreading major innovations through imitation and copying in the business world. While there is an advantage to being a first mover, many corporations have made a good living

by following the leader, often improving the product or production process to society's benefit.

Society benefits tremendously from new technologies—new products and production processes—coming from relatively small investments in research and development. General support for all R&D is important, but two areas would seem to be especially significant for our future, namely basic research in energy (both new sources of energy and the efficient utilization of energy) and ecology. Unfortunately, the US has been spending a lower portion of its GDP on basic R&D than some other countries, and much of our current spending is on military applications.

FEDERAL TAXATION. The USA is a high-expenditure and low-tax nation, prone to running large fiscal deficits that cannot be maintained in the long run. We need to cut government spending on national defense, our major health programs (Medicare and Medicaid), our direct and indirect subsidies to business (especially in the areas of alternative energy and corporate agriculture). As an alternative, we could increase taxes. We could:

- raise tax rates,
- reform our tax system by eliminating popular tax deductions (which we discussed as tax expenditures in Chapter Seven), or
- impose a new value added tax (VAT), which is essentially a sales or excise tax on the production of goods and services.

Economists generally would prefer to cut expenditures a little, reform the tax system, and impose a VAT. They feel that a VAT is superior to other taxes because it doesn't reduce incentives for people to work, save and invest.

The ratio of our National Debt to our annual Gross Domestic Product (GDP) drifted down from over 70% to below 60% under President Bill Clinton, who was the last president to have a fiscal surplus. The ratio drifted up about 5% to nearly 65% under George W. Bush. It then skyrocketed to nearly 100% in the first term of Barack Obama. This does not mean that we should place all the blame for this turn of events on President Obama because:

---

1. The Great Recession, which necessitated large fiscal deficits, started at the very end of George W. Bush's term in office. The causes of the financial collapse actually took place in Bush's eight years.
2. President Obama also inherited two wars from President Bush.
3. President Obama's three controversial stimulus packages, which created huge fiscal deficits, were probably necessary to keep the American economy out of a depression (This verdict is controversial among professional economists.)

Economists believe that when the national debt to GDP ratio reaches 90% to 100%, a country could face difficulty financing further large fiscal deficits because investors don't want to hold its debt obligations (long-term bonds and short-term Treasury bills). This is why large fiscal deficits, greater than the long-term growth rate of GDP, cannot be sustained indefinitely.

THE ROLE OF GOVERNMENT

REGULATION. Liberals support free enterprise and our market economy in theory, but don't trust business people and want to regulate them in practice. During President Obama's first administration the number of regulations and regulators increased significantly, especially in the areas of homeland security and the environment. Some analysts believe that fear of regulation has been a major reason why the business sector has been unwilling to invest more in spite of the fact that it is holding huge amounts of cash assets. I have three comments about government regulation:

- Europe has a lot of labor market regulation that limits the ability of business firms to fire or lay off workers and imposes large employment taxes on employers. This has been a major cause of a low rate of economic growth, a very weak recovery from recession, and a high rate of unemployment, especially of young people, throughout much of Europe. America's labor market flexibility has helped us avoid similar problems. Hence, we definitely do not want to follow Europe's lead in this area.
- We need fewer rules and more incentives to change business behavior. For example, if you want less pollution from cars, tax their emissions, raising the price of the worst offenders relative to clean and green ve-

hicles. You could even use the taxes raised from high-pollution cars to subsidize the production and sale of low-pollution cars. This is a far more effective way to achieve your objective while reducing the need for enforcement and a large bureaucracy. (This is the economist's way of achieving worthwhile social objectives. It would work for all kinds of ecological concerns, including increasing the energy efficiency of automobiles by increasing gas mileages.)

- There is one area that needs more regulation, not less—large financial institutions. Banks that are "too big to fail" and need government financial guarantees in a financial crisis, like that of 2008, must be either broken up or heavily regulated to prevent them from taking too many risks. We should use progressively higher tax rates as banks and other financial institutions grow in size; this would allow those with sufficient scale economies to remain large, but give most big institutions a strong incentive to break themselves up, reducing the risk that America and the world will suffer through more major financial crises like those of 1929 and 2008. (There have been many major disruptions between those two dates; financial crises occur regularly because too many financial institutions are allowed to become "too big to be allowed to fail.")

STABILIZATION. It is a primary function of the federal government to use fiscal and monetary policies to stabilize the economy by preventing inflation and recession in the short run while promoting economic growth in the long run. While there is no disagreement about our objectives, there are major institutional impediments to our ability to achieve our stabilization goals. Let's look at two of them and discuss how they could be improved:

- Fiscal and monetary policies have become one-way instruments that are used primarily against recession and almost never against inflation. If the unemployment rate rises a little or the economy dips into a mild recession, the administration, Congress and Federal Reserve Board all are ready to come to the rescue with more government spending, lower taxes, faster growth of the money supply, and lower interest rates. But when inflation occurs, everyone is prepared to "let the good times roll" until the rate of inflation becomes unbearable or the economy suffers a financial crisis. Expenditure cuts, higher taxes, less monetary growth and higher interest rates are nowhere in sight. And we can forget about any concern for the long-term rate of economic growth as the orientation of our policy makers is exclusively short-term. The view is that, after all, in the long run we are all dead.

- The monetary authorities—the Federal Reserve Board—do not seek to keep the economy within the narrow band, letting it fluctuate a little with its self-correcting mechanism. Rather, they seek to keep the economy at the upper limit of the narrow band. They do this by keeping interest rates low no matter what. They have a banker rather than an economist orientation, focusing almost all their attention on the financial sector rather than the overall economy—on interest rates rather than GDP and the level of unemployment. The result is that they destroy half of the economy's adjustment mechanism, the one that works through interest rates, business investment, and spending on consumer durables. (The other is the automatic stabilizers that work through employment taxes, unemployment benefits, and welfare payments.)

I will always blame the Fed for the financial crisis of 2008. In the long run-up to the collapse of the housing and mortgage markets, the Fed kept interest rates abnormally low and the money supply growing faster than real GDP. Key people saw problems but did nothing to prevent the disaster. They literally "let the good times roll" until collapse was inevitable. Were there other villains? Sure, one can talk about big financial institutions taking too many risks (which the Fed could have stopped), about regulators not doing an adequate job (including the Fed's own regulators), and about politicians wanting everyone in America to be able to own their own home, whether they could pay for it or not. If you believe that the monetary authorities were not culpable in the 2008 collapse, explain to me why the Bank of Canada, with powers that are similar to those of the Fed but with a better sense of economic restraint, kept our northern neighbor out of similar difficulties.

WHAT CONCERNS ME

There are eight major problems that concern me but which are not dealt with explicitly in this book. Four of them are world-wide in scope and four of them are primarily American in nature, although many other countries have somewhat similar problems. The four world problems are these:

GLOBAL WARMING AND ECOLOGY. To believe that mankind is not affecting the world's ecological systems is to fly in the face of scientific evidence and projections. Yes, it is possible that the world is going through a cycle that is causing a rise in temperatures. However, it seems almost a certainty that mankind is doing things that are amplifying the cycle, raising serious questions about the future of the planet. Conservatives, in particular, need to get their collective heads out of the sand and stop distrusting scientists and their evidence.

This is being written just after Hurricane Sandy hit the US in late October of 2012. Is it just a coincidence that the largest, not the strongest, storm in our history occurred at this time? Given the scientific predictions that such storms were going to be happening with much greater frequency, I don't think so.

RESOURCE DEPLETION. Our world has vast quantities of many natural resources—vast but not infinite. Some of our key resources are renewable, but most are not. America and other advanced nations use scarce resources with little concern for the future. But now the Less Developed Countries, led by China, are growing rapidly, using more scarce resources. World demand is rising but supply is finite, so price is rising. We are not running out of anything yet, but we can expect the cost of acquiring many natural resources, including several agricultural staples, to rise over time.

NUCLEAR PROLIFERATION. Nuclear proliferation is taking place at two levels—nuclear energy and nuclear weapons. Both are creating a major problem of dealing with nuclear waste. The latter is creating a separate problem of international political instability. What does the rest of the world do when faced with such unpredictable and unstable countries as Pakistan, North Korea and Iran having nuclear weapons capability?

TERRORISM. There are three dimensions to the terrorist threat:

- There is a definite possibility that terrorists could acquire nuclear weapons from either Russia or Pakistan. An even bigger possibility is acquiring biological and chemical weapons from a far wider range of sources.

- International terrorism has made being abroad in many parts of the world, for either work or travel, hazardous for Americans.
- Domestic terrorism is becoming a greater threat, especially with the internet providing ready access to information about terrorist organizations, their methods and making weapons.

The four primarily American problems are these:

EDUCATION. The quality of American public education at the primary and secondary levels is far too low. Our students are falling farther behind those abroad. Our public schools cannot compete with private, parochial and charter schools. The litany of problems includes the following:

- The curriculum has been dumbed down and deemphasizes the essential basics of mathematics, science and English.
- Ethnic minorities have lower than average academic performance and graduation rates.
- The turnover of teachers—especially the better and younger ones—is far too high because of low pay and disenchantment created by restrictions on what can be done in the classroom.
- Teachers' unions protect tenure systems and seniority-based pay scales while resisting performance standards and incentives.
- Students and parents are treated more like adversaries than customers by the educational establishment.
- Public education has become bureaucratic, becoming top heavy and not putting enough of its scarce resources into the classroom.
- Textbooks and what is being taught have become way too liberalized and politically correct.

American higher education also has problems, especially with high costs and the need for remedial classes for so many of its entering students, but at least it retains its rank as the best in the world, although the gap is narrowing and other countries are gaining.

CULTURE. Our culture is changing and many of us of different political persuasions believe that it is doing so for the worse. We see such things as the breakdown of the two-parent family, the decline of civic associations, and the deterioration of faith in God and our religious institutions. We see too many of our people addicted to electronic devices, food, medications, drugs, pornography and gambling. We see dishonesty and a loss of personal ethics in both business and government. We see too many people avoiding productive work and living on the government's teat. We see life as becoming far too impersonal as people seem less willing to sacrifice for or cooperate with others. We see rights taking precedence over responsibilities and instant gratification replacing long-term commitment. We see the loss of what liberals call virtue—the combination of character and competence— in our public officials and a corresponding decline in citizen interest and participation in the political process. And we wonder if America has begun a steady decline into mediocrity, following the other great civilizations into the dustbin of history.

WATER. Except for its upper northwest corner, the American West is a vast arid region. It has a rapidly growing population, major industrial interests, and a large agricultural sector. The Colorado River feeds seven states with most of their water needs but is so over-committed and overdrawn that it rarely reaches the sea. It has ten major dams and eighty major diversions. The legal battles over water rights are legendary. It relies on snowmelt from the Rockies, but there is growing concern that such is declining because of a long-term cyclical downturn coupled with global warming. The Sierra Nevada Range provides water for northern California, but much of that is siphoned off by canal to feed the big cities on the southern coast and agriculture in the Central Valley. Once again, the decline of the snowmelt is raising alarm bells. Meanwhile, there are such diverse water problems as the Sacramento Delta facing salinity and underground aquifers everywhere having falling water levels and even drying up, causing subsidence.

THE LEGAL SYSTEM. America was supposed to have a constitutional balance of power among the legislative, executive and judicial branches of government. Liberalism has given us judicial supremacy with an all-powerful Supreme Court that has been writing its own law and remaking America. Liberal constitutional thinking has achieved its two major goals of equality and liberty. The former extended equal protection of the law to everyone, seen in rulings against discrimination, for affirmative action, and for one man, one vote. The latter is far more controversial because it defined the liberty guarantee as assuring individual autonomy—the right to make important decisions without any interference and to define one's own concept of the good life. This gave us the abortion rulings. The major questions now facing our society are these:

- How far should liberal activism be allowed to go in the courts?
- Can and should the liberal versions of equality and freedom be contained?
- What are the current limits of government jurisdiction and domination, and what should they be?

WHAT WE HAVE LEARNED

At the end of a major project like this, an author must ask himself two questions:

- What has he been trying to say to his readers?
- Has he been successful in laying out his major points?

In answering the first question, I came up with an even dozen key ideas that I have tried to convey to you. I thought I would again share them with you, the readers. I will leave it to you to answer the second question. Anyway, here are the twelve points:

1. Populists correctly feel that there is something wrong with our economy, society and politics, but they have no program to improve the situation. Whether right wing or left, most of them want to return to a simpler day and age.

2. Libertarians have popular views favorable to personal freedom and hostile to government. Their policy is to reduce the size and scope of government and trust in free market mechanisms. However, they come across as so extreme that nobody but true believers takes them seriously.

3. Liberals have come to dominate policy, and have used it to seek and often achieve increased economic wellbeing, security and freedom for individuals in the lower income groups. However, while the overall results may have been positive for many individuals in the short run, they have often created problems for society as a whole in the long run.

4. A liberal society requires virtuous leadership—a combination of competence and character. Because of liberalism's emphasis on individual choice and aversion to promoting standards of morality, liberal soci-

ety has great difficulty developing leaders with the needed attribute we call virtue.

5. Although diverse, most conservatives believe in free markets, absolute standards of morality, and a well-defined but limited role for government. However, they are better in opposition to liberal programs than in formulating and instituting their own public policies.

6. A free market economy with a relatively limited economic role for government is superior to a directed economy with a dominant government. It provides a higher average standard of living, a higher rate of economic growth, economic freedom, and efficiency in giving consumers what they want. It can be criticized for its tendencies to create instability, inequality, insecurity and some forms of inefficiency. It is these problems that create a meaningful role for the public sector.

7. A market economy is subject to minor fluctuations in the short run but is inherently stable in the long run. However, it can be destabilized by major economic shocks which are usually, but not always, caused by inappropriate public policies.

8. Fiscal and monetary policies are relatively ineffective in preventing recessions and inflations because of long and variable time lags, moderately weak effects on the private economy, and an inherent inflationary bias. A major part of the problem is not that those in authority don't know what should be done, but rather that they seem unwilling to take action when needed.

9. Reducing the size of government isn't easy. At the federal level, 88% of expenditures are on national defense, Social Security, health care and interest on the national debt. At the state and local levels, 84% of expenditures are on education, health care, welfare, protection (police, fire and prisons), transportation, pensions and interest. That doesn't leave much. If you advocate a smaller government, you must answer the question as to what specifically you want to cut.

10. Contrary to original intent, a liberal judiciary and Supreme Court have successfully furthered the liberal agenda by eliminating religion from public life, increasing the power of the federal government relative to state and local governments, enhancing individual rights and freedoms at the expense of our social institutions and business

community, and reducing most forms of economic risk through a growing welfare state.

11. For liberals, vulgarity, abortion, gay marriage, pornography, and pre-marital sex are freedom issues for the individual, who is the focus of liberal attention. For conservatives, they are moral issues for society as a whole, which is the focus of conservative attention. Such differences in viewpoint are irreconcilable.

12. The greatest dangers facing America today are internal rather than external: the decline of morality, the decline of individual responsibility relative to collective rights, the decline of the middle class, and increasing social and economic inequality.

Finally, I asked myself whether all this could be brought together in a single, sweeping summary statement, a closing thought. This is my response:

We live in a liberal society, and that is a good thing. We should all enjoy our liberty, our tolerance, our generosity, our openness, our equality, our democracy, our free market economy. No, there is nothing wrong with liberalism. The problem is with liberals. They are never satisfied. They always want to go too far. Liberty turns into license. Tolerance becomes being politically correct. Generosity mutates into welfare. Openness creates illegal immigration. Equality goes to the extremes of similar economic outcomes. Democracy changes into sameness. Free enterprise gets regulated. And all of this is the very essence of America's problems.

FOOTNOTE:

1 "The Most Expensive Weapon Ever Built"; Time; 2/25/2013; pp. 26-31

www.ingramcontent.com/pod-product-compliance
Lightning Source LLC
Chambersburg PA
CBHW070646290526
45790CB00001B/196